"In *Grounded in Grace*, Jonathan and practical ways to have conversations with our children that will help them flourish by embracing their identity in Christ. Parents, your children need you to read this book!"
Darby Strickland, CCEF Counselor and Faculty

"Jonathan Holmes rightly challenges and encourages us to consider the ways we allow all the wrong influences to shape our kids and shows us how pointing them back to the Lord liberates them to truly be who they were created to be."
Julie Lowe, Counselor; speaker; author of *Safeguards*

"There may be no more important issue facing parents in our day than how we help our children discover the biblical answer to the question: *Who am I?* I'm urging parents I know who have teenagers and preteens to read *Grounded in Grace* by Jonathan Holmes."
Bob Lepine, Pastor, Redeemer Community Church, Little Rock, AR; author; longtime cohost, *FamilyLife Today*

"Jonathan Holmes's book, *Grounded in Grace,* is a wonderful blend of biblical insight and practical wisdom on this most personal subject of identity. A gift for parents in our confusing age."
Brian S. Rosner, Principal, Ridley College, Melbourne, Australia; author of *How to Find Yourself: Why Looking Inward Is Not the Answer*

"The genius of this book is that it takes the complicated (and vitally important) topic of identity and makes it understandable and it also equips parents to engage with their children in ways that are real, honest, and above all, biblically faithful."
Steve Midgley, Executive Director, Biblical Counselling UK

"*Grounded in Grace* offers vital direction amidst today's confusion about identity formation. Each page offers biblical truth and compassionate wisdom to guide families through the maze of insecurities and influences children face."
Eliza Huie, Director of Counseling, McLean Bible Church, Vienna, VA

"Reading this book will not only help you be more prepared as a parent but better equipped as a Christian."

Rebekah Hannah, Director of Kids and Families, Redeemer LSQ; President & CEO, Anchored Hope Virtual Counseling

"I hope every parent in my church gets a copy of *Grounded in Grace* to be equipped for teaching and training their kids in some of the most pressing and significant topics that kids and teenagers are facing today!"

Kyle Hoffsmith, Pastor of Family Ministry, Old North Church; board member, Center for Parent/Youth Understanding; podcast host, *The Word in Youth Ministry*

"This informative and practical resource empowers parents to engage in compassionate conversations with their kids about identity. Through relatable stories and thought-provoking questions, Holmes points to a gospel-centered identity with grace as its foundation."

Shauna Van Dyke, Founder & Biblical Counselor, Truth Renewed Ministries; strategic advisor, the Association of Biblical Counselors (ABC)

"Not only does Jonathan Holmes identify common challenges to our children's identity formation, but he shows how the gospel of grace gives kids eternal clarity amidst their temporal confusion."

Christine Chappell, Author of *Midnight Mercies*; host, *Hope + Help Podcast*; certified biblical counselor

"There may be no more important topic Christian parents can focus on right now than their kids' identity formation. The stakes are high on this one. *Grounded in Grace* covers this topic thoroughly, biblically, and practically."

Monica Swanson, Author; podcast host

"In *Grounded in Grace*, Jonathan Holmes looks at our modern identity crisis among teens and provides clear, biblical, and practical wisdom to the most common identity problems kids face today."

Courtney Reissig, Author of *Teach Me to Feel: Worshiping Through the Psalms in Every Season of Life*

"*Grounded in Grace* is a timely resource that equips parents to biblically shape and actively participate in their children's formation with joyful confidence and hope."

Joe Keller, Council Member, Biblical Counseling Coalition
Heidi Keller, Primary School Educator

"With front-row knowledge of the identity struggles of young people today, Jonathan Holmes provides parents with a biblical foundation and the practical help needed to engage adolescents in grace-filled, heart-level conversations about identity and worth."

Kristen Hatton, Counselor; author of *Parenting Ahead*

"Every parent would benefit from the wisdom that this book brings to the hot-button topic of identity."

Jeff and Sarah Walton, Authors of *Together Through the Storm*

"The joy and freedom of identity in Christ can be found throughout these marvelously practical and profoundly helpful pages. This book is essential reading for parents, educators, coaches, and youth ministry leaders."

Matt Koons, Associate Head of School, Cuyahoga Valley Christian Academy
Sara Koons, Kids and Students Director, Christ Community Chapel

"Jonathan Holmes provides a roadmap for parents to guide their children through a myriad of challenges and ultimately to find their identity in Christ."

Bob Butts, Chief Operating Officer, Truth for Life
Heidi Butts, Assistant to Head of School, Heritage Classical Academy

"This book will equip you to subvert untrue identity narratives and ever-shifting cultural paradigms about sexuality with gospel truths that each of us was created to know and live out of."

Jenny Solomon, Cofounder, Solomon SoulCare; author of *Reclaim Your Marriage: Grace for Wives Who Have Been Hurt by Pornography*

"This book provided clear and concise breakdowns of different areas of children's lives and how to support and disciple them through whatever comes their way."

Annie Roshak, NCAA Division II Elite Eight Most Outstanding Player and all-tournament team

"Holmes's tactic is sincere and clear as he writes from a professional counseling and parenting perspective. This book is an invitation to see our identity in Jesus as ongoing work—as we find our identity in God's grace, we can walk alongside our kids to help them see they are children of God."

Bailey T. Hurley, Author of *Together Is a Beautiful Place*

"*Grounded In Grace* is an invaluable resource for parents, as well as youth pastors and Christian educators navigating the complexities of discipling children in today's rapidly changing society. This book will be a source of strength for you as you parent."

Lia Ross, Christian book reviewer, @liarossreads

GROUNDED IN GRACE

Helping Kids Build Their Identity in Christ

Jonathan D. Holmes

New
Growth
Press
newgrowthpress.com

New Growth Press, Greensboro, NC 27401
newgrowthpress.com
Copyright © 2024 by Jonathan D. Holmes

Cover Design: Faceout Books, faceoutstudio.com
Interior Typesetting and E-book: Lisa Parnell, lparnellbookservices.com

ISBN: 978-1-64507-464-9 (Print)
ISBN: 978-1-64507-465-6 (eBook)

Library of Congress Cataloging-in-Publication Data
Names: Holmes, Jonathan D., author.
Title: Grounded in grace : helping kids build their identity
    in Christ / Jonathan D. Holmes.
Description: Greensboro, NC : New Growth Press, [2024]
Identifiers: LCCN 2024013799 (print) | LCCN 2024013800 (ebook) |
    ISBN 9781645074649 (print) | ISBN 9781645074656 (ebook)
Subjects: LCSH: Christian children—Conduct of life. | Group
    identity.
Classification: LCC BV4571.3 .H68 2024 (print) | LCC BV4571.3
    (ebook) | DDC 242/.62—dc23/eng/20240520
LC record available at https://lccn.loc.gov/2024013799
LC ebook record available at https://lccn.loc.gov/2024013800

Printed in the United States of America

31 30 29 28 27 26 25 24   1 2 3 4 5

Contents

Dedication

To Ava, Riley, Ruby, and Emma

I love you with all my heart.
Never forget who you are and follow Jesus no matter what.

Part 1

A Tale of Two Identity-Formation Processes

Chapter 1

Identity Formation: Who Are You and How Did You Figure It Out?

There is perhaps no more pressing a topic than identity.
—Carl R. Trueman[1]

Emma turned off her phone and buried her head in her pillow to cry. Her mom, Christina, lightly knocked on the door.

"Everything okay?" she asked.

"I don't want to talk right now," Emma replied.

"Okay, well, I'm here if you do want to talk."

"I hate my life; everyone in my grade is at homecoming tonight, and I'm stuck here without a date."

Christina sat on Emma's bed and tried to console her. "Oh Emma, why are you saying that? You didn't want to go to homecoming. Did something change?"

"I don't know. Nothing in my life is going right. I don't like my classes, and I'm failing geometry. Plus, someone at school is spreading crazy rumors about me," Emma cried.

"What kind of rumors?" Christina asked with a rising level of concern noticeable in her voice.

"I don't want to talk about it. It's so embarrassing. I just hate my life, and I feel so overwhelmed. Can you and Dad just homeschool me?"

Christina laughed out loud at this point. "Are you being serious, Emma? You told us you would never want to homeschool.

What's going on? You seem all over the map lately! You just don't seem like your happy self anymore."

Emma replied, "I don't know. It's all just so confusing. There's so much pressure to keep up with everyone. Every time I tell myself it's not a big deal, I just get more and more confused. I don't even know who I am most days."

THE PERENNIAL PROBLEM OF IDENTITY

Most parents I speak with and counsel are having conversations like the one above (or versions of it) on a consistent basis. In my current role as an executive director of a large counseling center, I meet with many parents who are trying to work through identity issues with their children. I hear stories and concerns from youth pastors, youth ministry staff, and Christian school teachers and administrators about the challenges they are facing in the local church and classroom. Our children are under enormous pressure to figure out who they are in an environment and culture that is sending them conflicting messages.

"Stand out, and be who you want to be!" *but* on the flip side we don't like who you are choosing to be and we're going to make fun of you for it.

"Live your own truth, and don't let anyone take that away from you!" *but* if someone else's truth contradicts "your truth," our teens are told that those individuals are dangerous and toxic.

"Who cares what other people think about you? You do you!" *but* you do need to care what other people think about you because you need their approval.

Conversations about identity have varied from generation to generation. For the baby boomers (1946–1964) and Gen Xers (1965–1979), one's identity was often tied to what a person did. The millennials (1980–1994) are a bit of a bridge generation in that more traditional ways of forming identity began to give way to more of a modern understanding of identity. Gen Zers (1995–2012) have distanced themselves from those earlier generations. Whereas previously identity was rooted in what you did, now for many, gender identity is what you feel yourself to be. If all of this is a bit confusing, hang tight as we explore this in greater detail in this chapter and the next.

YOUR ROLE AS A PARENT

As you consider how best to walk alongside your child as they try to figure out their identity, it's probably helpful for you to start with an understanding of what the word *identity* encompasses. Here's how counselor Todd Stryd defines identity:

> Identity is generally understood as a person's sense of self or self-understanding. In the broadest scope, a person's identity is the collection of characteristics that make up who they are. These include personality traits, abilities, strengths and weaknesses, and likes and dislikes, as well as ethnicity and nationality, group affiliations, appearance, socioeconomic status, roles, value systems, and worldview.[2]

Put simply, when we are talking about identity, we are talking about what makes *you* you!

As we have seen, discussions of identity are complicated because people choose different foundations on which to base their identity.

So where should our children turn as they seek their own identity? A biblical understanding of this endeavor is that our child's identity must be rooted first in an understanding of who God is and what he has created us for and to be.

The greatest problem our kids are facing regarding the issue of identity is this: an anemic and even nonexistent notion of who the Lord is and what he has called us to be. Stryd continues, ". . . a true and complete human identity must include our status as a child of God and citizen of God's kingdom. This aspect of a person's identity is in fact the most fundamental—it holds all the rest together."[3]

It shouldn't surprise you that it is my belief and conviction that parents[4] are God's chosen ambassadors for this most important work of identity formation (you did pick this book up after all!). You are given the task and stewardship of helping your child grow up in the nurture and admonition of the Lord (Ephesians 6:4). Parents play the formative role in the development of their child's identity. Whether we like it or not, our voice is often the loudest voice in our child's heart and mind as they seek to figure out who they are. Brian Rosner writes,

> Parents knowing their children is particularly important for a child's sense of identity. Parents not only reflect back to their children their identities but also play a big role in forming those identities. Children are named by their parents and receive their earliest experiences from them. Parents pass on their own tastes, values, and worldview to their children. Indeed, parents play a big part in the formation and maintenance of their children's identity, especially when they are young.[5]

Over the next few chapters, my hope is that parents can understand the challenges our kids are facing related to developing, maintaining, and resting in their identity. However, the contents of this book will be beneficial for a variety of individuals who are teaching and discipling children and teens: youth workers, Sunday school teachers, Christian school workers, and Christian counselors. In this chapter and the next, we'll look at two views of how identity is formed—the traditional view and the modern view—and explore the historical development of each one. Strengths and weaknesses of each will be assessed, and a third way will be proposed. Additionally, this material will be helpful for a variety of other individuals who provide discipleship, care, and instruction for children. Whether you are a small group leader in your church's youth group or a Sunday school teacher, the information contained here will help you answer questions and provide solid, biblical hope in a variety of situations.

In subsequent chapters, we'll dive into five different areas where kids and teens tend to struggle with their identity:

1. Academics
2. Sports
3. Moralism
4. Gender
5. Sexuality

Chapters 3–5 will describe areas where kids build their identity on what they do, and chapters 6–7 will describe how kids build their identity on how they feel.

As you consider your child or teen, perhaps you have seen that they struggle in one of these areas or several of these areas. In each chapter, we'll explore the struggles our families are facing, the heart issues at play, and practical, gospel-centered conversations that can direct our children to the truth of who God says they are. Because there is overlap in what causes these various struggles as well as how parents can address them, I recommend that you read all five of these chapters, even if your child seems to be wrestling with only one of these issues.

But before we dive into the specifics, we need to get oriented to the current landscape of identity formation. If you are unfamiliar with terms like *identity formation*, a glossary is located on page 105 to help define and explain words you'll find in the book.

TRADITIONAL IDENTITY[6]

Historically, identity was formed in response to the question, "Who do you want to be when you grow up?" Most children would have responded with something to the effect of, "I want to be a good person. I want my parents to be proud of me." Making parents proud was one of the most important things to a child, and it was accomplished by fulfilling the role that a son or a daughter should play in society.

In traditional settings, a son was to follow in the vocational footsteps of his father. If your father was a baker—guess what—you'd be a baker. If your father was a farmer—guess what—you'd become a farmer. Career days at the local Anglo-Saxon elementary school would have been boring and predictable.

For daughters, there was even less mystery or variety. In traditional settings, the role of a daughter was to get married, have lots and lots of children, and be a submissive wife. No dual-income households or moms who homeschooled and then moonlighted on the side as a business professional. No, daughters were raised for one primary role.

Why was this so? Well, historians tell us that this push to live a good and honorable life was ingrained in society. Early philosophers like Socrates, Plato, and Aristotle believed there was some moral good in the universe (represented by virtues like love, justice, honor, and fidelity) that the individual should align themselves with.

For boys, the ultimate realization of this would have been to die in battle for the good of your family, tribe, and clan—think Mel Gibson in *Braveheart* or Russell Crowe in *Gladiator*. For girls, the ultimate realization of this would have been less exciting. You guessed it—the goal would have been to have a large family (preferably sons) and be a loving and submissive wife.

How was success determined in a traditional identity setting? Well, ultimately one needed the approval and affirmation of an outside authority, namely one's parents. Parents or a higher authority were the ones to say, "Well done. You have brought honor to the family."

MODERN IDENTITY

Somewhere along the way, a shift began to take place in the culture. In modern identity, the determiner of identity has moved from something outside of you to something inside of you. Your inner voice is now the decisive factor of determining who you are and what you want to be.

Nineteenth-century philosopher John Stuart Mill sums up the prevailing philosophy well: "Over himself, over his own body and mind, the individual is sovereign."[7] The sovereign self is exactly that. You do you—you live your best life, an authentic life. In a modern identity context, the highest pursuit is the individual's happiness and well-being, not the happiness or well-being of the family, tribe, or clan. To live an authentic life is seen as the highest good.

How did this shift happen? Well, it took place steadily post-Reformation. In the 1600s–1700s, Enlightenment thinkers like René Descartes and John Locke wrote that there is a moral good that we should align ourselves with; however, they didn't go to the Bible or tradition to find or define it. No, they said we can rationally determine in our own minds what is right and wrong. Pushing the envelope further, Romantic thinkers like Jean Jacques Rousseau (1700s–1800s) wrote that it's not just our reasoning that determines what is right and wrong—it's our feelings. We have to dig deep into our feelings to determine what is good.

Rousseau writes, "The individual is at his best—he is most truly himself as he should be—when he acts in accordance with his nature."[8] Now, in our postmodern society we have taken this reasoning and accelerated the implications. Not only do we determine our own identity, we can conform and contort our physical bodies to align with what we perceive and feel ourselves to be. Feminist author Camille Paglia states it bluntly, "Fate, not God, has given us this flesh. We have absolute claim to our bodies and may do with them as we see fit."[9]

Another way to trace the development of identity might be like this:

Traditional Identity	Identity is predetermined and earned
Modern Identity	Identity is discovered as you reason and feel it

HOW MODERN IDENTITY MAKES ITS WAY INTO OUR HOMES AND FAMILIES

As a father to four girls, I am well attuned to the magical world of Disney. From their theme parks to their movies to their global empire of products, Disney is a shaping influence for many. Now hear me rightly: I'm not anti-Disney or advocating for a boycott of Disney, but rather, I want to show you how the modern (postmodern?) process of identity formation we described above makes its way into our homes and into our children's hearts.

Take a moment and think with me about some well-known Disney characters. Take Elsa in *Frozen*, for instance. Elsa's parents die in a tragic storm and leave her to rule in their stead over the kingdom—a classic traditional identity paradigm. It doesn't matter what Elsa feels like doing, what she must do is what her parents tell her to do. Throughout the movie, Elsa feels this internal conflict deeply, but eventually her feelings about who she is ultimately win the day. In her breakout song, Elsa talks about breaking free. What is she exactly breaking free from? The old, traditional ways of constructing identity. She's tired of suppressing her true self; she wants to live out her true identity.

Another example is *Moana*, Disney's foray into the lovely world of Polynesia. Moana's parents have clear plans for her—rule the island in their stead—but Moana has other ideas. Moana wants to be an explorer. She wants to launch out on a boat and see what is beyond her tiny island. Similar to Elsa, Moana feels an internal conflict as well. The battle is between what her parents desire for her and what she feels she wants to be.

Moana could just play her expected role and fulfill her parents' wish for her and be who they want her to be. But her feelings and internal voice are telling her something different. She wonders what's wrong with her. Hopefully this isn't too much of a spoiler, but guess what Moana chooses? You got it. At the end of the day, Moana chooses her feelings and internal intuition.

sake of illustration. In the newest, live-action remake of *Aladdin*,
Jasmine's father, the sultan, wants her to get married to a handsome young prince—a very traditional course of action that
would ultimately place her on the sidelines. But Jasmine doesn't
want to. In one of the moments from the movie, Jasmine belts
out that the old way of doing things is behind her, and now she
is embracing her own voice. No longer is she going along with
old-fashioned and antiquated rules and roles. She wants to be
free to speak her mind.

Again, I'm not anti-Disney in any way, but simply want to
show you how culture shapes and forms us through not only
the upstream of academics and intellections, but also the down-
stream of movies, social media, literature, and art. The new
understanding of identity is everywhere.

Is There a Third Way?

As we will see, neither the traditional model nor the modern
model works as the basis for a sure, godly identity. One process
(traditional) puts all the power of identity into the hands of one's
parents and family of origin, while the other process (modern)
locates it solely with the individual. So what are we to do? The
answer can't lie in a mushy amalgamation of traditional and
modern identity, but a true third way. Who better to turn to in
times when we need a true, stable, and secure word on who we
are as individuals than the God who made heaven and earth,
boy and girl.

We echo the words of Simon Peter who said, "Lord, to
whom shall we go? You have the words of eternal life, and we
have believed, and have come to know, that you are the Holy
One of God" (John 6:68–69).

As you read about modern identity, I'm confident you
see some of the immediate concerns with this identity formation process, namely that it is rooted in one's own feelings and
self-determination. You might be tempted to say something to
the effect of, "See, that's why we need to get back to the old way

of doing things—a time when kids respected their elders and parents." But we would err there too. While traditional identity has its positives, it has drawbacks too.

Timothy Keller writes, "The traditional self is suffocating, captive to what your family and tribe tell you that you must do. Adding some religion and moral structures only aggravates the problem."[10] Additionally, in a traditional identity formation system there is little to no room for the individual child to chart their own path that is different from that of their parents. What is wrong, for instance, if a child of a local farmer wants to be a teacher? Or if the young girl working at her parents' store wants to head off to university to study and become an engineer? While the subjectivity and permissiveness of modern identity has its own set of problems (we'll discuss five of them in the next chapter), the traditional identity formation process has its own pitfalls as well.

Bringing It All Together

What we need to pass on to our children, then, is neither an identity that they must earn from us (traditional) or an identity that they must create for themselves (modern), but an identity that is received and not achieved. A gospel identity comes from outside of us and relies on the unchanging, steadfast words of a God who is the final authority. We do nothing to earn God's approval. He creates us in his image, redeems us from sin, and brings us into his family. The identity he gives us is bigger than ourselves, more permanent than anything we could ever imagine, and true today and forever regardless of our circumstances or situations.

Listen to the way Jesus frames this in Matthew 10:39: "Whoever finds his life will lose it, and whoever loses his life for my sake will find it." In modern identity our children are told to dig deep inside themselves to find themselves, and lo and behold, a generation is struggling in the end to find true meaning. The gospel, as it always does, turns things upside down. Jesus commands us to first lose our lives, and in losing our lives we ultimately find our identity in Christ.

What does Jesus mean when he speaks of losing our lives?

C. S. Lewis writes, "Give yourself up, and you will find your real self. Lose your life and you will save it. . . . Look for yourself and you will find in the long run only hatred, loneliness, despair, rage, ruin, and decay. But look for Christ and you will find Him, and with Him everything else thrown in."[11] The late John Stott echoes Lewis: "The astonishing paradox of Christ's teaching and of Christian experience is this: if we lose ourselves in following Christ, we actually find ourselves. True self-denial is self-discovery."[12] In other words, when we focus our energies and passion on discovering what God has called us to do, our very identity often takes care of itself as we find our meaning and purpose in him. What an amazing truth that we can pass along and live out before our children.

Similarly, a gospel identity protects us and our children from pride and self-reliance. Christopher Watkins explains, "The fact that we are in the image of God and are not God therefore prevents us from thinking too highly of ourselves. It also prevents us from assuming the burden of defining ourselves. It reminds us that we are not the final court of appeal in questions about our own identity. . . . I do not ultimately own or define myself."[13]

Do you see the freedom and the beauty of an identity that is received and not achieved? Do you see the relief that comes when we entrust our whole being to a sovereign, wise, and loving God? Here's another way to see the three systems of identity formation compared to one another:

	Traditional	Modern	Gospel
Where does my identity come from?	Familial/ Societal: my parents, tribe, or clan.	Individual: I choose who I am.	God gets the final say on who I am.
Who gives it to you?	Chosen for you.	You choose it.	Given to you.
What is the goal?	Being an honorable or good person.	Being an authentic person.	Being who God designed me to be: an image-bearer of the living God.
Who validates who you are?	Parents (some sort of human higher authority)	You do	God
What constitutes the core of who you are?	You are what you do.	You are what you feel.	You are an image-bearer of the living God.
What do you do with feelings and emotions?	Ignore them and stuff them away.	You are your feelings.	Feelings are a part of God's good design, but they don't rule you.
How do you relate to the world you are embedded in?	Fit in with what is expected of you.	Stand out and be special.	Be on mission for Christ.

This chart helpfully summarizes the differences between these three identity formation processes. In the next chapter, we'll discuss in more depth some of the pitfalls and problems of the traditional and modern identity formation process.

Chapter 2

Problems with the Modern Identity-Formation Process

If you believe the Gospel and all its remarkable claims about Jesus and what he has done for you and who you are in him, then nothing that happens in this world can actually get at your identity. Imagine, for a moment, what it would be like to believe this. Consider what a sweeping difference it would make.

—Timothy Keller[1]

In the previous chapter we discussed the two primary ways individuals have come to a sense of who they are: traditional and modern. While both systems have positive aspects to their formation process, the concerns far outweigh them.

Often when I go and speak with parents on this topic of identity formation, I'll have dads and moms come up to me afterward and say something like this: "That's why we've got to get back to the good 'ole days when kids obeyed their parents and did what they were told." Makes sense, right? Everything in our society would be better *if* our kids just listened and obeyed us. If they took their identity cues from their older, wiser parents.

But wait, Tim Keller says, "In the past vast numbers of people were locked into a given social status in extremely hierarchical societies where peasants were to stay forever poor simply because it was thought that one's identity was one's role in society. These hierarchies were justified as reflecting some cosmic order of spiritual and moral absolutes."[2] Not only that, but what if children are growing up with bad parents, abusive parents, absent parents, and so on? Do we really want children looking to *them* to form their core sense of who they are? There's no stability and security in that dynamic.

So while traditional identity might be the one that sounds most appealing to many parents because it relies heavily on your ability to control your child's sense of identity, that is far too much power for any flawed human—even a wise, loving parent—to wield.

Similarly, the modern identity formation process is fraught with problems too. We'll spend the balance of this chapter unpacking them in far greater detail, primarily because most of our children and teens are swimming in these cultural waters.

Think of the six problems discussed below as six potential pathways of interaction that you can have with your child about issues of identity.

PROBLEMS WITH THE MODERN IDENTITY CONSTRUCT[3]

The modern process of identity formation is incoherent. What I mean by that is this: if your identity is ultimately found by going into your feelings, you will be left with confusion and incoherence. Our feelings, while good, are not reliable enough to stake our entire identity on.

Nancy Pearcey writes about this in addressing the current controversy surrounding gender identity: "Though our feelings are important . . . they are not what define our identity. Nor are they a reliable guide to God's purposes. Because we are fallen and sinful, our feelings fluctuate over time. The most reliable marker of who we are is our physically embodied, God-given identity as male and female."[4] If we build our entire sense of who we are on our feelings, our identity will be incoherent on any given day when our feelings about who we are do not align with who we want to be.

For instance, there are many days I wake up and don't *feel* like going into work.

On April 15, I don't *feel* like being a taxpayer.

On any given day, I don't *feel* like being a husband, father, employee, friend, etc.

Conversely, on some days I wish and *feel* like I could be an NBA superstar or some New York City billionaire. However, just because I *feel* like I am those things—or should be—does not make it true or a reality. (Trust me, you do not want to see me play basketball.)

If my identity was primarily built on my feelings, I would be an incoherent mess! What happens if you can't make sense of your feelings? What happens to your children if they can't make sense of their feelings? How does that impact their sense and understanding of who they are?

The modern identity formation process is crushing

Not only is the modern identity formation process incoherent, but it is also a crushing burden to bear for the individual. In a traditional identity setting, the broader goal as it relates to society is for us to *fit in*: Don't make a fuss if you don't get what you want, just go with the flow. In contrast, modern identity pushes us to *stand out*.

No longer can a person be average or normal. Every child is told they must stand out and be special, unique, and one of a kind. I'm a longtime subscriber to *TIME* magazine. Every year they release issues throughout the year along the lines of "Top 100 Most Influential Adults" or "Top 40 Young People Under 40" and so on. The idea being *TIME* selects and curates people across the globe doing amazing work. As an adult, it's aspirational and inspiring. But what happens when the media starts spotlighting the most amazing *children* in the world? Then we move from aspirational and inspiring to crushing and overwhelming.

Consider Cash Daniels, age thirteen and self-styled environmental activist:

Daniels spends several hours every week cleaning up cans and bottles in the rivers with other teen environmentalists in Chattanooga, TN. Together, they have collected more than one ton of aluminum cans, nearly 1000 cans a week for a year. . . . he co-founded a club called the Cleanup Kids with his best friend, Ella Grace, a fellow home school student who lives in Canada. The two met at a three-day bootcamp in Vancouver called Ocean Heroes and now video chat almost every day. Together, they decided they will encourage kids to pick up 1 million pounds of trash across the globe before the end of the year.[5]

Now, please hear me rightly: I'm all for caring for our planet and stewarding it well. But listen to the conclusion that Cash reaches toward the end of the article: "But in truth the burden to save the planet has landed on children like him. 'Kids may be a small percent of the population, but we're 100% of the future,' he says. 'And we can save the world.'"[6]

Think back to when you were thirteen years old. What were *you* doing? I venture a guess that it's nowhere near what thirteen-year-old Cash Daniels is doing!

Articles like this, while reminding us of some of the wonderful and amazing things children are capable of doing, also remind us of the crushing burden of self-identity that can be placed at the footstep of the individual. The allure of determining one's identity brings with it a corresponding burden that is not easily discerned. Determining and maintaining our identity is a heavy load we were not meant to bear, and our children were definitely not meant to bear.

The modern identity formation process is enslaving

Modern identity promises autonomy, freedom, and self-assertion. It proudly and loudly proclaims, "Be whoever you want to be." But is that true freedom? Keller writes, "Defining freedom this way—as the absence of constraint on choices—is unworkable because it is an impossibility. Think of how freedom actually works."[7] In what way is this kind of freedom impossible? Think with me for a moment about freedom specifically when freedom is faced with conflicting choices and options.

This past summer our family went to Michigan where we have vacationed the past six or seven summer with dear friends of ours. The highlight of the summer vacation is what we lovingly refer to as "lake day." The day where we rent a boat and spend the day on one of Michigan's lovely lakes boating, swimming, and tubing. When we get in the boat and begin to head out into the lake, there are signs everywhere that tell us what speed our boat can go. This is done because the wake caused by our boat could cause a number of issues for nearby boaters and swimmers.

Additionally, as our families want to go tubing, we have learned that we get the greatest enjoyment out of speeding along the lake in the inner tube when we observe the necessary restrictions on how close we can get to the edge of the lake—because of the speed the boat is going, the design of the boat itself, and the safety of the riders. Note that the restriction actually maximizes freedom and enjoyment, not the other way around.

This hit home in a particularly poignant way just earlier this week for me as I visited my medical doctor for an annual checkup. My doctor noted that my blood pressure was consistently registering higher than she would like it. Along with a prescription medication, she also advised me to alter my diet, specifically limiting certain foods. Friends and family that know me, know I love anything salty or fried. (I confess that I'm a sucker for chips and French fries.) Coming out of the doctor's office, I am faced with a choice. I *could* eat whatever I want because it's my life, but I would be making a choice that would limit my health, my longevity, and ultimately my desire to grow old and see my children grow up, get married, and have children. The choice then is a fairly easy one for me: limit my freedom in one area so that I can experience freedom in other areas.

Similarly, modern identity promises freedom, but what it tends to do in the end is enslave the individual to the whims, wishes, and approval of the self and a watching world. While it trumpets freedom, it ends up trapping the individual in a prison of their own making. It's simply not realistic to always say yes to your desires and feelings. But that is what the modern identity formation process does. It puts the individual at the center of their universe.

The modern identity formation process is fragile

Although the modern identity can appear to offer positivity and strength, it is also surprisingly fragile. Think with me about this scenario: Sammy is a seventh grader at her public school. As she comes into her first period class, her teacher, Mr. Hall, passes out a letter to the class. In the letter, Mr. Hall announces to the class that Julia is trans, and is asking the class to now use his preferred name—Bobby—and preferred pronouns—he/him. This comes as a surprise to Samantha, who sits next to Julia (Bobby).

Later in the week, as Samantha is chatting with a friend, she mentions Julia's name. Her friend immediately corrects her, "Samantha! Don't you remember, Julia is Bobby now. We need to respect and affirm his new identity." Samantha blushes and hastily exits the conversation. Later that night at dinner she brings up the situation with her parents. Her parents listen and empathize with her predicament but are similarly confused as to how to proceed.

The next morning in class, Julia (Bobby) leans over to Samantha and whispers, "Hey, I heard you were using my old name. I really don't like that. Please use my new name and preferred pronouns." Later that day, Mr. Hall asks Samantha to stay after class, and he too relates that he has heard that Sammy is still using Julia's name and feminine pronouns. He reminds her of the announcement he read earlier in the week, and tells her, "We really need to respect Bobby's new identity and choice. When you use his old name and feminine pronouns, that's really harmful to him." Samantha nods, gathers up her books, and hurries out of the classroom.

What is happening here? *If* modern identity is something you choose, who cares what other people think about you? After all, isn't that *their* choice to make? Why impose the burden of affirmation of your identity on others if you yourself authenticate and determine your own identity?

But you see, therein lies the problem. Because in modern identity you determine who you are and then go out into society and demand acceptance, affirmation, and approval. But when that identity is not immediately affirmed and used (especially by Christians, for instance), there is significant pushback. Raising questions is deemed hateful and bigoted. Modern identity produces a need for external affirmation and validation.

The modern identity formation process is performative

Traditional identity was of course performative—you were expected to do certain things to gain the approval of your family and society. But the modern identity process is particularly performative. One must constantly perform before an audience for affirmation. The process begins with digging deep into our feelings to determine who we are, and then going out into society and performing said identity. At this point, society is required to offer not just affirmation for our chosen identity but engage in activism and endorsement as an ally.

In traditional identity, an individual did not need to earn or perform for their identity as much as they needed to simply fill the role that had been given or passed on to them from their parents. The irony is that in the modern identity formation process, even though you choose who you want to be, you also need the affirmation and approval of people around you to affirm who you are. This helps us understand today's need and motivation to be on social media so much. We now have unlimited and unfettered access to audiences who can affirm and approve of our chosen identity. Likewise, it's widely considered important self-care to cut out anyone from your life who chooses not to actively affirm your chosen identity.

The modern identity formation process is ultimately an illusion

The final problem with the modern identity formation process is that it is ultimately an illusion. In one of my favorite scenes from *The Devil Wears Prada*, Andy Sachs (played by Anne Hathaway) gets taken to task by Miranda Priestly (played by living legend Meryl Streep). In the scene, Andy snickers as Miranda and her cabal of fashionistas discuss the color difference between two seemingly similar belts. Miranda replies about Andy's sweater in a now-famous monologue, "That blue represents millions of dollars and countless jobs and it's sort of comical how you think that you've made a choice that exempts you from the fashion industry when, in fact, you're wearing the sweater that was selected for you by the people in this room from a pile of stuff."[8]

It's not often that our culture tells us explicitly how it shapes us, so pay attention to what Miranda is saying: while Andy might think she's making a choice for herself in choosing a certain colored sweater from a secondhand store, the color of that sweater was actually predetermined by a group of higher-ups in society. Andy didn't make the choice at all—it was made for her.

Los Angeles pastor and author Jeremy Treat states the situation well, writing, "It's interesting how being 'true to yourself' usually means aligning with some mainstream cultural narrative."[9] Ultimately, in modern identity, no one is *choosing* their own identity as much as that identity formation process has been *chosen* for them through countless cultural narratives and marketing campaigns.

Perhaps an even more obvious example of this dynamic hit home recently as I was speaking at a large youth conference. A junior girl and her mother came up after a talk I gave on gender identity, and she related a story to me. Her friends asked her, "Are you gay or straight?" The abruptness of the question surprised this girl, and she hesitated in answering. Immediately, her friend jumped in and said, "Oh, if you don't know, then you're definitely bi."

The girl and her mother were understandably distraught as now the rumor around school was that she was bi. This young lady didn't have a chance to defend herself or offer an alternative; she was quickly and efficiently deemed bi because that's what fit her friend's cultural narrative.

So how do we address these problems? If both the traditional and modern identity formation processes present us with such outstanding conundrums, how in the world can we ever figure out who we are, let alone guide and help our children to know who they are? The resounding answer to these identity formation processes is the good news of a gospel identity. A gospel identity meets and answers the challenges that modern identity creates:

- *Incoherent*: A gospel identity is coherent from the start. The truths of the gospel are unchanging and stable.
- *Crushing*: A gospel identity alleviates the need to "measure up" because our worth isn't tied up in what we do, but who we are in Christ!
- *Enslaving*: A gospel identity is freeing—it frees you from having to do whatever it is your feelings tell you to do.
- *Fragile*: A gospel identity is sturdy, strong, and steadfast because it's not built on something inside of us, but on the words of God himself to us.
- *Performative*: A gospel identity frees us from the trap of having to constantly perform for the approval of others because Jesus has secured our acceptance before God through his sacrifice on the cross.
- *An Illusion*: A gospel identity is a true reality. It places us securely within the story that makes sense of every other story.

Michael Horton sums it up well, "The Good News is not just a series of facts to which we yield our assent but a dramatic narrative that replots our identity."[10] The narrative of Scripture is the story we all need to make sense out of who we are. For it is in that story that we are told who we are, why we exist, what has gone wrong, what makes it better, and the final end we are all headed toward.

But while the good news of an identity that is received and not achieved makes sense to us, we must also account for the reality that we are limited as parents in our ability to convey and convince our children of the beauty of a gospel identity. Our theology aids us in this in remembering that it is ultimately the Lord who opens hearts and minds to the truth of the gospel (1 Corinthians 2:14; Ephesians 2).

BRINGING IT ALL TOGETHER

As parents we must ask ourselves how can we help our children grow and cling to what God has to say about them? How can we make the gospel attractive, like apples of gold in settings of silver? Todd Stryd writes,

> While parents can metaphorically set the table of formation by working to shape, direct, and educate them, children choose whether to take these things to heart. . . . As creatures with active, desiring, worshipping hearts, children have agency and choice. They must choose between life and death, foolishness and wisdom, righteousness and wickedness. So while parents must humbly recognize that they can't make their children "eat" and "digest" godly truth and wisdom, they can faithfully make the "table" attractive and the "food" appealing. To do this, parents will need to balance both flexibility and fidelity. Parents may need to adapt their tactics and tendencies while still remaining faithful to the general principles that God has called them to.[11]

We will endeavor to explore those tactics and tendencies in the ensuing chapters as we delve into various identity struggles that our children and teens are facing. In the remaining balance of the book, you'll meet five different kids who are all struggling through identity in various ways. The first three kids you'll meet—Neera, Marcus, and Josie—are building their identity on what they *do*: academic performance, athletic ability, and good behavior/moralism. In the latter two chapters, you'll meet Juan and Isabella, two kids who are building their identity on what they *feel*. As you read, keep what we have discussed so far in the back of your mind.

Remember, we do not want to divorce theology from practice. Otherwise we will unfortunately reinforce an identity formation process that is ultimately rooted in *our* powers, rather than resting in the power of God and the Good News. We want our children to know that at the end of the day, the most important voice they must listen to in the process of figuring out who they are is the voice of God. He knows them, loves them, and has created them for his glory and good purposes. Dr. Judy Cha aptly reminds us, "We need someone outside of ourselves who has the authority to give us an identity, someone who is both perfectly just and perfectly loving, who will never change his mind about us and who will give us an identity. We need a redeemer."[12]

Part 2

I Am What I Do

Chapter 3
Neera and Academics

Neera opened up her Chromebook and logged on to her Canvas account. As she scanned her progress report, she inwardly cringed. *Ugh . . . why is chemistry so hard?* As she peers through the coursework, she sees that her last lab assignment received a 90 percent.

Neera starts to cry, but through sheer self-control, she holds the tears back. That only makes the problem worse, and so throughout the day she ends up with a massive stomachache and headache from holding in her anxiety. She wonders to herself how she'll break this news to her parents as they'll inevitably see the latest progress report. Neera remembers last quarter when this happened and the look of disappointment on her dad's face.

ACADEMICS AND ANXIETY

Let's face it, the pressure kids are facing today related to academics is enormous. Nearly everyone acknowledges the negative and detrimental effect that COVID-19 had on students' academics. Researchers are telling us the students are falling behind in math, reading, and history. Test scores are much lower across the board in subjects compared to where students were scoring three years ago.[1] Kids feel pressure to get a 4.0 GPA in order to get into college, but even when they do, that is in and of itself not a foolproof guarantee of success as 40 percent of students who go to college do not even finish![2]

According to a 2015 study by Council of the Great City Schools, "The average student in America's big-city public schools will take roughly 112 mandatory standardized tests between pre-kindergarten and high school graduation."[3] "By contrast, most countries that outperform the United States on international exams test students three times during their school careers."[4] In addition, mounting levels of homework only increase the stress levels children and teen experience. A recent poll reported teenagers spending, on average, more than three hours on homework each school night, with 11th graders spending more time on homework than those in any other grade level.[5]

One mother commented on the pressure her daughter faces:

> From the start there is a grading system that focuses mostly on academics, and it is not a fluid system that takes into account strengths and weaknesses of each individual. They become recognized by their achievements, and there is a lot of attention put on being the smartest and having the highest GPA and being in honors classes so you can get into a good college. It's so easy for children to carry that and feel that is the only thing that gives them value or worth. It is a lot of pressure.[6]

I know that on a regular basis beginning as early as first grade, my children are undergoing days of testing; testing rigorous enough to merit a letter home to parents notifying them to feed their children a full and healthy breakfast in addition to written letters of encouragement to "do their best." I'm by no means an expert in education, but I simply seek to demonstrate the point that children face academic pressure that can adversely (or positively) impact their identity.

Here's how the internal thought process for a typical middle-schooler might play out:

> I have to ace this exam or at least get an A in order to pull out an A in this course. If I don't, then I won't qualify

for the AP course in 9th grade. Ninth grade is where grades really begin to count. Colleges look at my high school transcripts, so I have to make sure I get into the right courses my freshman year. If I don't, I'll probably land at some junior or community college. No one will want to hire someone with a junior college degree. Are you kidding me? Plus, my best friend is a straight-A student. She gets tutoring and SAT prep help every Saturday. I'll never be that good. Who am I kidding? There's no way I'll ace this exam. Guess I'll just have to settle for an A.

Whether you attend private school, public school, or are homeschooled, there is some level of academic pressure to perform from teachers and parents alike. What can parents do to disciple their children into a gospel identity, not an academically based identity?

How Can Parents Help?

Be aware of your own internal compass

As parents consider the pressure children are under with academics, perhaps the first thing we can do is to look in the mirror. Are we as parents creating a healthy environment and setting appropriate expectations when it comes to grades and academics? Are we making sure to separate academic performance from how we love and speak to them? One mother commented on the pressure she placed on her daughter as a result of her own family upbringing:

> I was the first in my family to attend and complete college with a four-year degree. I was identified by my academic achievements and scholarships. Without realizing it, I began to instill that drive into my child in an unhealthy way. I saw she was smart and could catch on quick, so I pushed hard to enroll her in harder, and more advanced classes without realizing that she

was struggling socially and mentally with the pressure of trying to live up to my expectations. I really believe in always learning and the importance of academics and doing well with whatever you try, but I have had to lessen my expectations depending on the season we are in and ultimately only caring that she put in the time and effort and did her best versus the grade and outcome.[7]

I must confess this is an area I continually struggle with. As a Korean American, coming from an ethnic culture and tradition that puts a high priority on grades and academic performance, I can create and foster unrealistic expectations surrounding school performance. One memory stands out to me. One of my children (whose identity I will protect), got a low B on an exam. My daughter knew I wouldn't be too pleased with such a grade, and she related this to her friend. Her friend jokingly replied to her, "That's like an Asian F!"

Now in some households I realize a B would be met with welcomes and cheers, but I had created an atmosphere through both spoken and passive comments relating that particular grade was not acceptable. It was only through the gentle counsel of my wife that I was able to reflect and realize I was placing an undue burden on my daughter as it related to her grades. Additionally, I realized it was less about what grades she made, and more about how that reflected on me. Thankfully, the Lord had mercy and helped me see my error.

Help your children see the flaw in building their identity on academics

Do you remember in chapter 1 how we discussed the differences between traditional and modern identity? One of the problems associated with how modern identity gets constructed and created is that it is so fragile and susceptible to the approval of others. This is acutely true when it comes to how kids can build their identity on academic performance.

If a child or teen places how they view themselves in how they perform at school, the opportunities for both sin and suffering abound:

- A junior in high school stays up late every night of the week studying for exams. The lack of sleep, in turn, brings about anxious feelings and a stressed body.
- An eighth-grade girl is trying to balance her homework and friends, but consistently she chooses her homework over her friends. Her friends, tired of being second choice, move on from her, leaving her alone and isolated.
- A young scholar-athlete knows he needs a certain grade in his high school trig class in order to compete at sports. When the chance presents itself for him to cheat on an upcoming exam, he takes it because of the immense pressure to perform.

Now hear me rightly: I'm not saying these various academic scenarios make your child sin or suffer, but the pressure presented by pursuing a certain level of academic acumen surely plays a significant role.

Parents, we must teach and talk to our children about academics, grades, and education in a way that promotes their identity in Christ while still encouraging them in their schoolwork. One way you can do this is to prioritize character formation over academic performance. What would it look like to help your child grow in the areas of diligence, humility, modesty, gratitude, and honesty?

Collaborate on expectations in order to build connection

We hear a lot in parenting books and resources about the need for connection and attachment between parents and children. Parents can help build connection with their children through collaboration. Sometimes we can set expectations related to academics that can unintentionally signal to our children that our approval and affirmation is tied into those expectations.

Conversely, our children often have internal expectations themselves (as evidenced by Neera's example above) related to academics. The conversation cuts both ways. Ideally, parents work with each child individually to come up with expectations that are appropriate for that child's unique gifts and challenges. What might collaboration look like with your child or teen on this topic? Perhaps a sample conversation like this could get you started:

> "Hey, is this a good time to talk?" (Note that we are seeking to have them participate and collaborate in the process from the beginning!)

> "I was wondering if we could chat about your school schedule, grades, and classes this year. How are you feeling about this year?"

> "What do you remember about last year? How do you think it went? What would you do differently?"

> "Are you feeling some pressure this year? What could I do to be helpful for you?"

Wade through heart issues

Does your child or teen enjoy conversation? If they're like mine, the answer might be yes or no depending on the day, the time, the weather, the . . . well, you get the point. Conversation with kids today can be more challenging because of smartphones and decreased attention spans. When it comes to grades and academics, finding the right time and focusing on heart issues is important for parents who want to move the conversation from mathematics to motives.

Why does your child struggle with finding their worth in a grade? Why is pursuing a 4.0 so important to them? Why do they seem crushed when report cards come out? These questions and many more are all in need of exploration. Perhaps seeing them as such could be a powerful source of connection with your child or teen, rather than a source of consternation or discomfort. I find several motives can be at play in the heart of a child.

POSSIBLE MOTIVES IN THE HEART OF A CHILD

Approval of their parents

As we've covered above, parents can be a significant source of pressure on children to perform academically. While dispensing rewards and consequences based on grades might make sense to us, we need to be aware that our children might not make those connections or discern those distinctions. For instance, a parent might reason to themselves, "I want to offer a reward for hard work and excellence at school by giving $40 for straight As on a report card." The child might interpret this as, "My dad *only* rewards me when I get perfect grades." Or perhaps a parent offers a later bedtime on a holiday weekend if their student brings their math grade average from 70 to 80.

Note the intent behind the parent's reward and the interpretation the child comes away with. As parents, let's be clear in our communication that rewards for particular academic achievements will be given, but our approval of our children is not ultimately tied to their performance.

Affirmation from their teachers

The majority of teachers I have had the privilege of knowing are passionate about teaching and education. For many students, elementary in particular, the desire to please one's teacher is natural. Students often will come home saying things like, "When I grow up, I want to be like Mrs. _____." Teachers play an important role in our child's life.

Because grades play an integral role in the educational life of the child, it is entirely plausible for a child to want to get good grades, assuming that is what will make their teacher happy. I don't know of many teachers who are *dis*pleased with good grades, so the connection is easy to make for kids.

A child might desire the affirmation and approval of their teacher to the point where they beat themselves up over getting a poor grade on an exam or assignment. They might create an internal narrative in their heart that their teacher doesn't like them because of a grade they received. As Paul Tripp has often been quoted saying, "A good thing becomes a bad thing when that desire becomes a ruling thing."[8] We will want to help our children understand that receiving the approval of their teacher is good but not the most important thing.

Accolades from their peers

For some children, the pursuit of academic excellence is tied to the praise of their peers. Stereotypes abound of the dumb jock or the nerdy academic, but we know in real life these caricatures rarely hold up to scrutiny. Many athletes excel in academics and many academics excel in athletics. The idea that kids who make good grades are made fun of might be rooted in pop culture or stereotypes, but it is also equally possible that kids who make good grades and excel in academics receive affirmation from their peers.

A more frequent occurrence are children and teens who experience a need to constantly compare themselves and measure themselves against their peers, especially as it relates to academics. Report card time and end-of-the-year grades can become opportunities for both jealousy and despair.

Anxiety about the future

We've discussed the ways that anxiety from a variety of audiences can spill over and impact the student. Whether the audience is parents, teachers, or peers, many students develop struggles with anxiety. One particular direction anxiety can take is anxiety about their future.

Questions surrounding their academic performance and their ability to potentially qualify for scholarships is a dynamic that increases as they go through high school and near their graduation date. When I was a high school student (admittedly ages ago), I went through a normal high school educational program with no AP courses or college-preparatory courses. Today, more and more high school teens take heavy loads of AP and college-prep courses to get a leg up in the college admissions race.

Students can now complete significant portions of their undergraduate degree requirements while in high school. Many do this to save money; others to help them expedite their educational trajectory. Anxiety can play a significant influence in this.

- *Will I be able to get a job after college?*
- *What will my major be?*
- *Are my grades good enough to qualify for that scholarship?*
- *Will I have to go to community or junior college?*
- *How will I be able to afford college if I don't get a scholarship?*
- *What if I can't get into the school I want?*

One of my daughters has a thought process something like this: *I have to get good grades to go to college. If I can't get into college, then I'll end up working at a fast-food restaurant.*

Bringing these questions and concerns into the light can be helpful in hearing the student's internal processing and narrative. Remember, thoughtful question-asking (not the interrogation kind) can be a helpful way to know our kid's hearts (Proverbs 4:23).

Angst about themselves

The final heart motive that could be a potential driver for a student who finds their identity in academics is personal angst about themselves. If the dominant narrative in our culture is that you are your performance or you are what you make yourself out to be, then the flip side of such a narrative is surprisingly bleak for some. What happens when your student comes home with a C in Geometry? Or they score a 1200 on their SATs? Or they don't pass their AP exam? What does that communicate to them when they have built their identity on excelling in academics?

A frequent contributor to the angst that some children and teens experience is all-or-nothing thinking. All-or-nothing thinking operates something like this: a child or teen creates an academic goal that is either pass or fail. There's no in-between here. If the goal is to get a 100, then there is no grace for a 99 or an A-. Students who struggle with this kind of thinking tend to set internal goals and expectations that become difficult to dislodge.

One mother I spoke with about this noted how she has engaged this thinking with her child:

> Once I noticed my teen was struggling with perfection-ism and all-or-nothing thinking patterns, I had to con-tinue to remind her that academics and grading are just one way to observe if a student is learning material and not the only way to show strength in a particular sub-ject or concept. I had to (have to still) remind her that God has created us with so many different talents and gifts and strengths and part of growing up and learning is figuring those things out. It's always more important to me that I teach kindness, teachability, and humil-ity, rather than only being concerned with academic progress.[9]

Understanding the heart of our child is what we are called to do, but it's not always an easy thing to do. Whether the motivation is

- Approval of their parents
- Affirmation from their teachers
- Accolades from their peers
- Anxiety about the future
- Angst about themselves

Parents will do well to see the motives that are driving their children's harmful behaviors and address and engage those with compassion and creativity, reinforcing the truth of how the Lord sees them regardless of their academic performance.

TEACH EARLY, TALK OFTEN

Parents are called to be the primary disciplers of their children's hearts. If you're reading this and you are a single parent, this calling is for you too! God can use single parents, divorced parents, and married parents for this work of discipleship. What matters is a heart that is ready and willing to live out this calling.

Listen to what Moses charges the people of Israel with in Deuteronomy:

> "Hear, O Israel: The Lord our God, the Lord is one. You shall love the Lord your God with all your heart and with all your soul and with all your might. And these words that I command you today shall be on your heart. You shall *teach* them diligently to your children, and shall *talk* of them when you sit in your house, and when you walk by the way, and when you lie down, and when you rise. You shall bind them as a sign on your hand, and they shall be as frontlets between your eyes. You shall write them on the doorposts of your house and on your gates." (Deuteronomy 6:4–9, emphasis added)

Notice that discipleship is to have both formal (teach) and informal (talk) aspects to it. The beginning point of discipleship here is clearly laid out: children must understand their ultimate *purpose* in life, which then informs the *meaning* of life. A child's purpose in life is to know and love the Lord their God with all their being. How does this inform the meaning of life for kids? Well, if a child understands that their ultimate purpose is to know, love, and treasure the Lord above all things, then it protects them from ultimate despair when other secondary purposes in their life don't turn out how they want them to.

Think of this imperative offered in Deuteronomy as the top button of a shirt. When the top button is buttoned correctly, it allows the rest of the buttons to line up and properly be buttoned. If you get the top button askew and start in the middle, for instance, you'll have a mess on your hands! *This is the top button: loving God with all their being.* Academics? Yes, it's important, but it's not top-button important.

As Neera battles internal angst over her chemistry exam, the truth of who she is and what she is ultimately called to do can help guard against her sense of self being completely unmoored by a bad grade on an exam.

Let's imagine a conversation between Neera and her father, Arun:

Neera: "Papa, I'm really anxious about my chemistry grade. I looked at my last lab assignment grade, and I don't think I scored high enough to keep an A in the course."

Arun: "Oh, Neera. Come here, my love. Chemistry is rough. I remember how hard my chem teacher was in high school. I dreaded going into that class. Do you remember what we've talked about though as it relates to your grades?"

Neera: "Yes, but there's so much pressure on me!"

Arun: "I know, I know. I can't imagine how much pressure you and your friends face today. But remember you are more than your grades and academic performance. We want you to do your best, but the most important thing is your relationship with the Lord. There are a lot of young ladies out there who are making straight As and getting into Ivies, but inside they are unhappy and unfulfilled."

Neera: "You're right, and I know that, but it's so hard!"

I'm confident as a parent you have been here before with your children. Pastor and author David Murray sums it up well, "Perfection is impossible in this world, and it is a tyrannical master. So let's not impose that upon our kids. If we have to choose between a 4.0 GPA and a healthy teen, let's make sure we choose the latter."[10]

BRINGING IT ALL TOGETHER

When I think about the pursuit of academic excellence, the apostle Paul comes to mind. Listen to his academic résumé as it were:

> Though I myself have reason for confidence in the flesh also. If anyone else thinks he has reason for confidence in the flesh, I have more: circumcised on the eighth day, of the people of Israel, of the tribe of Benjamin, a Hebrew of Hebrews; as to the law, a Pharisee; as to zeal, a persecutor of the church; as to righteousness under the law, blameless. But whatever gain I had, I counted as loss for the sake of Christ. Indeed, I count everything as loss because of the surpassing worth of knowing Christ Jesus my Lord. For his sake I have suffered the loss of all things and count them as rubbish, in order that I may gain Christ and be found in him, not having a righteousness of my own that comes from the law, but that which comes through faith in Christ, the righteousness from God that depends on faith—that I may know him and the power of his resurrection, and may share his sufferings, becoming like him in his death, that by any means possible I may attain the resurrection from the dead. (Philippians 3:4–11)

Paul had the résumé of résumés. He would have been a National Honor Society, valedictorian, full-ride to Harvard University guy. But . . . Paul says that whatever good that résumé entailed is nothing compared to the *surpassing worth of knowing*

Christ. Because Paul knows Christ and his identity is secure in Christ, he is able to say this to the Corinthians:

> Moreover, it is required of stewards that they be found faithful. But with me it is a very small thing that I should be judged by you or by any human court. In fact, I do not even judge myself. For I am not aware of anything against myself, but I am not thereby acquitted. It is the Lord who judges me. Therefore do not pronounce judgment before the time, before the Lord comes, who will bring to light the things now hidden in darkness and will disclose the purposes of the heart. Then each one will receive his commendation from God. (1 Corinthians 4:2–5)

It is astounding that Paul valued his view of himself in Christ more than his impressive academic résumé. It would have been easy for someone like Paul to turn his nose up on the comments and opinions of his detractors and haters because of his academic prowess, and yet that's not what he bases his response on. Author Chris Morphew gives some additional insight:

> Paul said he'd found a way to stop being overwhelmed by everyone's opinions (he didn't really care if they judged him) and to stop beating himself up about his own failures and weaknesses (he didn't even judge himself).

> How did he do it?

> It wasn't just by ignoring his haters and being true to himself—he knew that even if his choices seemed right to him, that didn't necessarily mean he was innocent.

> Paul discovered this freedom by finding another place to turn for love and acceptance and significance—another voice to help him figure out who he was and how he should live.

For Paul, true freedom came from finding his identity in who God said he was.[11]

You see, our child or teen's identity and ultimately even salvation does not come from how well they perform on an exam or what university they get accepted to. Their identity and worth come from another. It comes from knowing and being in relationship to the perfect, righteous Son of God, Jesus Christ. Jesus came to earth, lived a perfect life, died a horrible death, and he rose victorious over death. The exam came, and he passed it with flying colors.

Imagine an academic setting where your child, for free, could have someone take an exam or test for them on their behalf and receive a perfect grade? Notice, I said *imagine* because as far as I know that never happens in the real world. And yet, in the storyline of the Bible, that's exactly what happened.

As parents, we must steward the influence and position we have in our child's life. Our words and our posture toward them heavily influence the internal voice, beliefs, and values that they grow up with. May the Lord help us to be parents whose words help reinforce and mirror who the Lord is and what he says about us.

Chapter 4
Marcus and Athletics

M arcus stumbled into his mom's car, dripping in sweat from the evening's basketball practice. As he shoved his bag into the back seat, he took his headphones and put them over his ears. His mom, Makiah, poked him in the shoulder.

"You going to thank me for picking you up tonight?" she said in jest.

Marcus pulled away and mumbled something under his breath.

"Hello! I'm talking to you!" his mom said, her voice rising this time.

"I don't want to talk right now. Can't you see that?"

"Why are you talking to me like that? I drove here after my evening shift! You could have just gotten a ride with one of your friends," Makiah replied, now irritated.

"I'm sorry, I'm just tired. Practice sucked. We are not ready for Friday's game against St. Johns."

"What do you mean? You guys beat them by fifteen points last time you played them."

"Yeah, when we had Marcus playing point guard. He's out with a sprained ankle, and now Coach wants me to fill in for him. I've never played that spot before, and I don't think I can do it. We're probably gonna lose, and the team is gonna say it's my fault," Marcus huffed.

"Whatever! You're gonna be fine. No one knows how to play basketball like you do," Makiah said confidently.

"You don't get it. It's a lot of pressure," Marcus shakes his head.

The world of athletics is one that touches nearly every American household in one way or another. Seventy-five percent of families have at least one child playing an organized sport. An estimated sixty million children (6–18 years of age) participate in sports. High school sports in and of itself is a nineteen-billion-dollar industry.[1]

Families face the demand to enter their child into sports at earlier ages than ever before. An athletic director at a well-known Christian university notes that as children enter sports at earlier ages, the chances of them refining their skills also increases. What this often leads to is burnout in athletics rather than increased joy and participation. He notes, "Their skills are refined at an earlier age. But we also see them starting to leave sports at the ages of 12 and 13 because they're burned out. . . . Early specialization, too, leads to earlier burnout."[2]

Couple that with the rising amount of pressure that student athletes are facing, and it's no wonder that an entire diagnostic label has come into our language: *sports performance anxiety* (SPA). There are many signs and symptoms of performance anxiety, and no two athletes will experience the same exact things. Signs of performance anxiety include feelings of weakness, "butterflies" in the stomach, elevated heart rate, fast breathing, muscle tension, frustration, paralyzing terror, cold sweat, clammy hands and negative self-talk.[3]

Recently, I asked a group of parents whose children play sports—elementary, junior high, and senior high—their thoughts on the current scene of athletics and whether there is pressure to excel and find one's identity in sports. Here are the answers I got:

There is tremendous pressure for children to excel in athletics in today's world. Sports have been glorified as one of the premier ways to ensure your child is in the "in" crowd, is recognized within the community, and is getting the glory you did or did not get in your own sports endeavors as a child. College and professional athletes are glorified to such a high degree in our culture: there is power, prestige, money, sex, and overall image. Everyone wants it—and their child is the ticket.

Yes, I do believe there's pressure on children to excel in athletics, especially here where we live, attending a large Division I school district. Whether the pressure is external or self-imposed from the children, I see it even as early as age eight. There are so many kids involved in every sport that there definitely is pressure to perform and to be a starter to play more and to make a travel team. I do see the performance anxiety in my children, I do see the self-imposed disappointment when they feel like they haven't performed well, and I see them tying their self-worth up in that far too often.

Yes. There is very little space for recreational athletics in middle school and high school. Despite the vast majority of high school athletes not obtaining college scholarships for athletics, many sports demand almost exclusive time and effort in both the season and the off-season. If an adolescent is interested in multiple sports, it becomes an even more life-dominating and high-pressure scenario. Anything less than this level of time and effort is considered a lack of commitment by many coaches and parents.

THE WORLD'S MEASUREMENT OF OUTWARD ABILITY: A BIBLICAL EXAMPLE

Our propensity as human beings to measure a person by their outward appearance or ability is nothing new. There's something about an individual's external appearance and abilities that lure us into equating that with worth and meaning. One of the more notable examples in Scripture comes to us in 1 Samuel, where Samuel, in searching for a replacement for Saul, seems perplexed that God doesn't go for the natural and logical option of Eliab to fulfill his spot. Eliab, Jesse's oldest son, would have been the logical choice as evidenced by Samuel's remark, "Surely, the LORD's anointed is before him" (1 Samuel 16:6).

We can infer to some degree that in addition to being Jesse's firstborn, he also physically presented himself as an obvious choice. Perhaps in feeling the need to find a replacement for Saul, who Scripture notes was both handsome and tall (what a combination) (1 Samuel 9:2), Samuel felt like Eliab could fit the bill. Yet, the Lord tells Samuel:

> "Do not look on his appearance or on the height of his stature, because I have rejected him. For the LORD sees not as man sees: man looks on the outward appearance, but the LORD looks on the heart." (16:7)

The Lord's admonition to Samuel is one we must keep in mind. What the Lord ultimately looks at is the heart. The heart in Scripture is the central part of who we are. It is the seat of our thinking, behavior, feelings, and will (Proverbs 4:23). That is what the Lord sees. Now, that does not mean that our outward appearance is of no concern or should be of no priority to us, but Scripture orients and orders how we prioritize and see the inner man and the outer man (2 Corinthians 4:16).

How Can Parents Help?

Pay attention to the pressure

The pressures children and teens are facing today seem markedly different from the pressures parents faced when they were growing up. Social media has opened up a world of ideas and values that are difficult to combat when kids are spending upward of eight to nine hours a day on social media apps. When you are consistently and constantly bombarded with footage from the best athletes in the country, it can feel as though you have to measure up to their level of performance. Additionally, pressure from parents, pressure from friends, pressure from total strangers all can play into our children's drive to find their identity in their athleticism. One athlete captures this dynamic perfectly:

> I have been playing competitive sports my whole life, and this [finding my identity in sports] is still a fight that I am constantly battling. I think that this happens for a lot of reasons. A lot of people start sports at a young age before they may truly grasp the concept of the gospel. Sports becomes their life at a young age, and it is so easy to wrap your worth and purpose in a little ball or on a field.
>
> There is instant gratification if you win, and it can seem like the end of the world if you lose. Sports are an easy thing for most people to talk about, so it can feel like all you are ever doing is talking about the game last night or what's coming up on the field this weekend. When children and teens are constantly surrounded by talk of "good game" and "who you got this weekend," it can be so easy to think that that is all people see you as and hold on to that super tightly.

Empathizing with your kid about these pressures can be a starting point for further dialogue. Sometimes, simply acknowledging what they are facing can help them feel seen and heard. In dialogue with your child, trying to pinpoint where some of those pressure points lie can help you better understand their struggle.

- *Internal*: Is some of the pressure to perform athletically coming from inside? Is there a certain expectation you have as it relates to this season/game?
- *External*: Is any pressure coming from you (parents)? Social media? Friends? Coaches?

Make sure this is a dialogue, and not an interrogation. Most kids don't enjoy what can be perceived as an investigation or an interrogation. Perhaps your children offer up bland responses to your questions: "I don't know . . ." When this happens, I remember a helpful tip from counselor and author Julie Lowe. Julie says when your child says "I don't know," simply respond with "Well, if you did know, what do you think you'd say?"[4]

Acknowledge the anxiety

We noted earlier that sports performance anxiety is a new category to describe a cluster of symptoms surrounding children and teens who struggle in sports. Children today report anxiety as the number one issue that brings them into counseling, outpacing depression for the first time since 2010.[5] It is estimated that anywhere from 30 to 60 percent of athletes struggle with some form of anxiety.[6]

Anxiety and depression are treatable, but 80 percent of kids with a diagnosable anxiety disorder and 60 percent of kids with diagnosable depression are not getting treatment, according to the 2015 Child Mind Institute Children's Mental Health Report.[7] Research shows that untreated children with anxiety disorders are at higher risk to perform poorly in school, miss out on important social experiences, and engage in substance abuse.[8]

One of the ways, I help parents understand anxiety and their child is by discussing the W-A-S cycle:

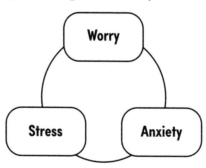

Figure 1. The W-A-S Cycle

This diagram helps parents visualize what may be going on in the life of the child. Worried thoughts produce anxious feelings, which causes stress in the body. Now if you use the terms *worry* and *anxiety* somewhat interchangeably, that is fine; this is just a helpful tool to help you and your child work out what's going on internally.

A sample dialogue between Marcus and his mother, Makiah might play out like this:

> Makiah: "Hey, what's going through your mind right now? I can tell something is bothering you."
>
> Marcus: "Nothing. I don't want to talk about it right now."
>
> Makiah: "Okay, are you sure? I'm here for you if you wanna talk."
>
> Marcus: "It's just a lot of pressure right now. Between school and my grades and basketball, it's a lot right now!"
>
> Makiah: "I know you've been under a lot of pressure! I've seen it too! How is all that pressure making you feel?"
>
> Marcus: "I dunno. Overwhelmed, I guess? Making me second-guess myself a lot. I thought I could handle the pressure, but for some reason, I'm stressed to the max for this game. I just don't want to be blamed if we lose."

You can see that through some persistence and simple questions, Makiah was able to move from worries to anxieties to stress, understanding Marcus's situation a bit better. This sense of everything riding on his shoulders is a lot of pressure to face.

This method of asking questions is the way of Jesus himself. In Matthew 6:25–34, the portion of the Sermon on the Mount in which he addresses being anxious, Jesus asks over half a dozen questions. I try and remind myself here of Jesus's tone. Is it a tone of reprimand? Condemnation? I don't think so. I think he genuinely wants to draw people to place their worries and anxieties, and ultimately their identity, in him. The questions Jesus asks are meant to draw us in and comfort us with the answers we already know to be true.

Know the narratives

Kids and teens who believe their identity and worth is tied up in their athletic abilities or performance often believe certain narratives that need to be brought to the surface. What are some of those narratives, and how can we draw them out?

For some kids, there can be an unspoken sense of expectation that they need to be the best athletically to make their parents happy. Or that they need to fulfill their parents' athletic dreams. We've all heard anecdotal stories of athletic parents seeking to live out their athletic dreams in their children. For some kids it can be playing in the same sport as their parents or achieving the same athletic records as their parents.

Our desires as parents can inadvertently become ruling expectations that our children believe they have to live up to although the desires in and of themselves may not be wrong or sinful. Listen to how one parent put it when asked about the way their desires can play into their child's identity:

> In my experience, the greater issue is parents that find *their* identity in being the parent of an athlete. You can imagine the pressure that a child may feel when their parents' identity rests on their athletic performance. It is no wonder that it becomes the thing they value most and begin to see as their identity/worth.

> It is often the strongest connection point between them and their parents (and sometimes even grandparents). There is a very fine line between proudly supporting your child/grandchild (which is healthy) and making sports the most powerful connection point in your relationship (which is so unhealthy).

I admire this parent's honesty in their final observation about sports being a powerful connection point for relationship.

There's nothing wrong with a parent and child enjoying sports or playing together, but as a parent are we cognizant and aware of when this becomes too central?

Additionally, some kids and especially teens believe their athletic performance is the key to a successful college career. Roughly 2 percent of public school athletes go on to compete in college, and $3.6 billion is handed out in athletic scholarships![9] Compare that with academic scholarships where the Department of Education alone hands out an estimated $46 billion in academic scholarships.[10] Despite those stats, many high school teens view their athletic performance and abilities as the ticket to college scholarships, when perhaps academic success may present a more balanced opportunity for accessing scholarship monies.

The allure for kids of playing, not only at the college level, but at the pro level is equally enchanting for some. Through the influence of social media, pro athletes have direct access to children and teens, demonstrating a lifestyle of wealth and freedom that is quite alluring for many. According to the NCAA website, "Of the nearly 8 million students currently participating in high school athletics in the United States, only 495,000 of them will compete at NCAA schools. And of that group, only a fraction will realize their goal of becoming a professional or Olympic athlete."[11] A local instructor at an elite golf academy in the Dallas-Ft. Worth area states it honestly, "If the kid enjoys the game, loves what they are doing, they want to do it, and they are out there, enjoying the heat of the competition, there's never enough for them."[12] It is this *never enough* mentality that feeds an outsized pressure on our children.

Face the failures

Children and teens who struggle with making their athletic achievements and performance the core of their identity,

understandably can be undone by failure. Failure can flesh itself
out in a variety of different ways:

- "I didn't score as many points as I had hoped that game."
- "I spent the entire second half on the bench."
- "I feel horrible that I am going to miss today's game."
- "This is the second year in a row we've been runners-up."
- "Coach won't even look at me, he's so disappointed."

Failures come in all shapes and sizes. Parents, we can help
our children understand that failure is a normal part of life in
a broken world. Things don't always go how we want them
to. Failure does not need to define me, and failures cannot be
avoided. Knowing this provides us with great freedom and comfort. Jesus, in a broad sense, affirms this reality in John 16:33
when he says, "In this world you will have trouble . . ." (NIV).

Remind them of the truth

My middle daughter, Ruby, plays basketball, and plays it
well (as I'm sure every proud dad says). On occasion her team
will play teams that are known to be better—with better players
and better records. When this occurs, some sports performance
anxiety can creep in. When this happens, I take her face, cradle
it in my hands, and tell her, "Whether you win or lose today,
I want you to know something. Your mom and I love you no
matter what, and God loves you too!"

Sometimes she laughs and giggles and rolls her eyes—
"Yeah, yeah Dad," she says. Repetition is key here. Each and
every time I have the opportunity, I want to reinforce simple,
but memorable truths. She is loved by her mother and me, and
she is loved by God. We need reminders of these truths.

In his second epistle, Peter reminds the believers on two different occasions of biblical truth:

> Therefore I intend always to remind you of these qual-
> ities, though you know them and are established in the

truth that you have. I think it right, as long as I am in this body, to stir you up by way of reminder. (2 Peter 1:12–13)

This is now the second letter that I am writing to you, beloved. In both of them I am stirring up your sincere mind by way of reminder. (2 Peter 3:1)

As humans, we are all prone to forgetfulness. I recently celebrated a milestone birthday, and I can tell you that the older I get, the more forgetful I become. Whether it's questioning why I opened a blank tab in my internet browser or wandering into a room and forgetting why I came, it's clear our memories fail us. This is true for our children as well. Although their memory can be more selective at times (e.g., "Remember that homework assignment that was due last Friday?"), the Lord knows that sometimes the most basic of truths are the ones we frail humans are most prone to forget.

As parents, what memorable ways can you reinforce your child's identity in Christ? Here are some suggestions that could be helpful to add to your repertoire:

- Regularly talk and tell your child truths about who they are—they are created by God, loved by God, and known by God.
- Find solid, gospel music that you and your child can sing together that reminds them of who God is and who they are. One of my favorites that comes to mind is from CityAlight, "Jesus, Strong and Kind."
- Pray with your children at night before bedtime and pray truth over them before the Lord.
- Find everyday, ordinary moments in your child's day where you can remind them of your unconditional love for them.[13]
- Consider working through a devotional, catechism, or book series that reinforces and reminds them of the truth.[14]

Bringing It All Together

Henri Nouwen writes about the five lies we all struggle with as it relates to our identity:

1. I am what I have.
2. I am what I do.
3. I am what other people say or think of me.
4. I am nothing more than my worst moment.
5. I am nothing less than my best moment.[15]

These lies are especially pernicious for those who are tempted to find their identity in athletic aptitude and achievement. The prevalence and perniciousness of lies like these make it all the more important for us as parents to help our children move their focus from one race to another race: the race of our Christian faith.

Scripture abounds with metaphors that help expand our imagination for what it looks like to follow Christ. One of Paul's favorite metaphors is that of an athlete running a race (sounds like Paul would have been a great cross-country athlete). Believers in Christ are called to compete like athletes in the Christian race. Listen to how he describes it in 1 Corinthians:

> Do you not know that in a race all the runners run, but only one receives the prize? So run that you may obtain it. Every athlete exercises self-control in all things. They do it to receive a perishable wreath, but we an imperishable. So I do not run aimlessly; I do not box as one beating the air. But I discipline my body and keep it under control, lest after preaching to others I myself should be disqualified. (9:24–27)

We can hopefully encourage our children that the most important *athletic* event to compete in is the race that Jesus Christ has called us to. Games, tournaments, achievements, and medals are great to earn and fun to compete for, but nothing will ever compare to the imperishable medal of pursuing Christ.

Annie Roshak, a renowned women's college athlete with a NCAA Division-II national championship under her belt, sums it up well in a conversation we had over email:

> Something that I have had to remind myself over and over again is that my sport is something I do, it is not who I am. If everything that brought me joy or purpose is as fleeting as losing a game or missing a shot, then I am missing the point. My worth and purpose has to be tied to something bigger than a game. As I've gotten older, the game has given me an amazing platform to be able to share with others what I truly believe and that has been the biggest blessing through sports. Not the championships or accolades. And that is another thing I have to remind myself when the workouts seem never-ending or I just want to quit . . . that I have been given this for a reason and the way I use it can and should be God-glorifying.

As parents, may we impress upon our children to "press on toward the goal for the prize of the upward call of God in Christ Jesus" (Philippians 3:14). May we remember that this race we are running is hard and often challenging, but we do so with the knowledge that One has gone before us, leaving us with this hope:

> Therefore, since we are surrounded by so great a cloud of witnesses, let us also lay aside every weight, and sin which clings so closely, and let us run with endurance the race that is set before us, looking to Jesus, the founder and perfecter of our faith, who for the joy that was set before him endured the cross, despising the shame, and is seated at the right hand of the throne of God. (Hebrews 12:1–2)

Chapter 5
Josie and Good Works

Trust yourself and anything you do will be right.
—My fortune from a fortune cookie on July 19, 2023

The Bible is about identity.
—Klyne Snodgrass[1]

J osie sighed as she closed her Bible and journal. She checked her phone to take one final look at her homework for school this week. She carefully completed her Bible assignment from Bible class, shoved it back into her backpack, and pulled out her Algebra textbook to finish her next assignment. As she worked her way through her problems, Josie heard her mom call her down for dinner. She hurriedly bookmarked her textbook and went downstairs.

As Josie's mom dishes up dinner for everyone, Josie's dad asks Josie and her brother how school went that day. Mark, Josie's precocious little brother, mumbled through food that it was "good" (his stock response nowadays). Josie chewed her food, swallowed, and replied, "Good, could have been better."

"What could have been better?" Josie's dad asked.

"Well, I've got so much homework, plus I have that volleyball tournament this weekend. I guess I'm just a little stressed out. Oh, I almost forgot, I have to work in the nursery too this Sunday," Josie sighed.

"Wow, that sounds like a lot. Do you think you're trying to do too much?"

"Oh no, I like being busy, plus I need those nursery hours to fulfill my community service requirement for Bible class."

"Well, I'm glad you're volunteering on Sundays, but you're not just doing it for the community service hours, right Josie?"

"Oh no, I like the kids I take care of. It's a great deal for me too—I get to play with the kids in the class and get my community service hours taken care of. Check and check," Josie smiled.

THE SUBTLE DANGER OF GOOD WORKS

Some parents might read the brief anecdote and say, "I wish I had a kid like Josie!" Smart, dutiful, service-oriented, and articulate. What could be wrong with that? Nothing. Unless Josie believes those good works are the basis for her relationship with Christ and not the *overflow* of her relationship with Christ.

Increasingly, I see more and more upper elementary school students and teenagers struggling in their faith because their faith is ultimately rooted in their efforts and not Christ's work on the cross. I know from personal experience how easy it can be to slip into a Christian moralism that looks good on the exterior but leaves the interior just as dead as that of the next sinner. Paul writes in Ephesians that on our own we were "dead in the trespasses and sins in which you once walked" (Ephesians 2:1–2). It is only by God's mercy that we are saved and given new life: "For by grace you have been saved through faith. And this is not your own doing; it is the gift of God, not a result of works, so that no one may boast" (vv. 8–9).

What's so dangerous about a child building their identity on their good works and efforts? I mean, there are a lot of other *bad* things a child could build their identity on, right? (In fact, we've already covered several!) The problem is that building your identity and worth on anything apart from who God is and what he says about you is ultimately an exercise in futility. As we have said earlier, our identity is something we receive, not something we achieve.

THE SUBTLE DANGER OF RAISING A PHARISEE

Anyone who has read the Gospels knows that Jesus's interpersonal ministry often looks and sounds different depending on who he is speaking to. When he's with the Samaritan woman in John 4, his approach is tender, inquisitive, and ultimately convicting. When he's with Nicodemus in John 3, his approach is straightforward, honest, and even incredulous. All that to say that Jesus is a master at knowing his audience and attenuating to their needs.

In Matthew 23, we see Jesus in a brutally honest conversation. I say *brutal* because there's no other way to describe it. In speaking to the Pharisees, Jesus pulls no punches. He doesn't hesitate to call out their hypocrisy and spiritual deadness. In a series of eight "woe to you" statements, Jesus calls the Pharisees out. Let's listen in:

> "Woe to you, scribes and Pharisees, hypocrites! For you are like whitewashed tombs, which outwardly appear beautiful, but within are full of dead people's bones and all uncleanness. So you also outwardly appear righteous to others, but within you are full of hypocrisy and lawlessness." (Matthew 23:27–28)

Imagine coming up to the popular (yes, the Pharisees were the popular religious leaders of their day) teachers of the law and saying this to them! Jesus is bold and clear, and his message is too. Why does Jesus reserve some of his harshest, but most honest, words for the religious? How could these "righteous" and "moral" teachers of the day be described as "full of dead people's bones and all uncleanness"? Jesus comments that these teachers of the law appear outwardly righteous, but the reality is the polar opposite.

Let's visit another passage which sheds further light on Jesus's relationship with the Pharisees. After Jesus calls Matthew, the tax collector, as his disciple, the Pharisees begin to grumble and complain:

As Jesus passed on from there, he saw a man called Matthew sitting at the tax booth, and he said to him, "Follow me." And he rose and followed him. And as Jesus reclined at table in the house, behold, many tax collectors and sinners came and were reclining with Jesus and his disciples. And when the Pharisees saw this, they said to his disciples, "Why does your teacher eat with tax collectors and sinners?" But when he heard it, he said, "Those who are well have no need of a physician, but those who are sick. Go and learn what this means: 'I desire mercy, and not sacrifice.' For I came not to call the righteous, but sinners." (Matthew 9:9–13)

Jesus is calling the Pharisees out on the danger in their dependence on their own works-based righteousness. Is there anything that is more of an affront to the good news of the gospel, than to reject the very premise and foundation of the gospel: that you cannot save yourself?

Now, what makes works-based righteousness so tricky and sneaky is that as a parent it so easy to praise and affirm moral behavior. I mean, let's be honest . . . what parent wouldn't want their child to adhere to their rules, standards, and guidelines? Who wouldn't want a child that happily goes to church, volunteers in children's ministry, is an active member of the youth group, and gets good grades in school? But all of that would be for naught *if* our child's understanding of the gospel is, "I obey, therefore I am accepted by God."

To help us understand the gospel of grace, Pastor David Strain writes,

We no longer need to shape identity by our *performance*. Instead, we can say: "I am accepted and counted righteous in Christ. God looks at me in Jesus. That's where my identity comes from. My identity doesn't come from my success in business or from my promotion. My value and worth are not located in my accomplishments. It is not located in me at all. It is located in Him, in Jesus."[2]

Children who are raised in Christian homes will experience, Lord willing, a rich heritage and example of a life lived before the Lord and for the Lord. Yet, even in Christian homes, I find many children and teens can exhibit several symptoms when they seek to build their identity on their good works.

FIVE SYMPTOMS OF WORKS-BASED IDENTITY

Judgmentalism

One telling symptom of a child who struggles with basing their identity on their good works is judgmentalism. An identity that is built on personal effort—the effort to be a good person that earns God's favor—*needs* to judge others in order to maintain a sense of superiority. It's easy to point at the sins of others and ignore the sins in their heart, or at least rationalize and minimize their own shortcomings. Additionally, the sins of someone who is outwardly a good and moral person often lurk subtly below the surface in the heart rather than manifest themselves externally.

In the story above, Josie frequently will make comments about her little brother Mark's behavior. Recently, they were at Target with their mom, and Mark grabbed a toy off the shelf which launched a cascade of other toys to tumble off the shelf. Josie stepped in, batted Mark's hand away, and scolded him saying, "What's wrong with you! Stop touching everything. Can't you just get through the store without destroying it?" In an everyday moment like this, Josie's quickness to judge and scold obscures her own battle with her internal frustration and anger, and focuses it on her brother's behavior. Her anger and embarrassment reveal problems in her own heart.

Self-reliance

A second telling symptom from the disease of Christian moralism is a reliance on the self. Remember in chapter 1 where we discussed and described modern identity? One hallmark of modern identity is that it is created and generated by the individual. We typically think of modern identity as it relates to gender and sexual orientation, but echoes of the modern identity formation process is at work here too.

In effect, moralism says, "Your identity is based on your efforts and good works." Therefore, the moral individual must rely on their good works to sustain their sense of who they are. While the behavior of the moralistic person might not look as brash and unacceptable as that of someone pursuing a gender identity different from their biological sex, this outcome is equally troubling and infinitely more deceiving. The child who finds their identity in their good works will ultimately have to rely and depend on themselves.

Pride

The third symptom flows out of the previous one. Guess who gets the glory and praise when I rely and depend on my good works as the basis of my identity? You guessed it—me! Now, this is the subtle danger for a child or teen who finds their identity in their good works and moralism. Because good behaviors and actions look good—on the outside—they are typically praised and encouraged (even incentivized!).

When we reinforce through praise and affirmation a child's good works, we can *inadvertently* communicate to our child that their actions are the basis of our relationship with them or the reason we love them. Here's a simple equation that can illustrate how this computes in the mind of a child:

Child + good behavior and actions=Parents are pleased

Child + good behavior and actions=God is pleased

Here in this category, one can see the echoes of the traditional identity formation process coming into play. In this setting, the child earns their sense of who they are from their parents. Now, am I saying that praising or affirming your child is wrong? Of course not, but we need to be careful in conversation to identify and name that it is not our good works that gain God's acceptance. How might this play out in your home? Does it mean you can never praise your child or their behavior? Certainly not; however, do we teach and remind our children that ultimately our acceptance before God is not based on our work, but on the work of Jesus Christ? Consider both formal and informal moments where you can both teach and talk about this good news with your child.

Exhaustion

The fourth symptom of a child who finds their identity in their good works is that they will be exhausted. You see, if my identity is generated by my good works (self-reliance and pride), it will lead to a never-ending cycle of needing to do more, not less. Again, one of the problems with modern identity is that it makes you incredibly susceptible to the approval and affirmation of others.

The result is a non-stop feedback loop of good works followed by praise and affirmation followed by doing more good works to reinforce and sustain the child's identity and the approval of others. Sooner or later, the child—or more likely the teen—gets to a spot where they realize this identity formation process is *not* sustainable.

Self-doubt

The final symptom of a child or teen who finds their identity in their good works and efforts is that of doubt. What do I mean by that? Well, let's take Josie, for example. After years of building her sense of who she is on her grades, work at church, good behavior, and so on, Josie begins to wonder, *Have I done enough?* which leads to *Am I enough?* When we build our identity on what we *do*, at some point we realize deep down inside our soul that indeed we are building an identity that is pretty small.

Someone once said that a child wrapped up in themselves makes a small package. If our children choose to build their identity on their own actions, what happens when they are not good? What happens when they make bad choices or engage in bad behavior? How does that fit into their economy of understanding who they are? No one is perfect, and an identity built on good works is not big enough or sturdy enough to withstand the failures that will inevitably come. That's where doubt creeps in and questions about being "good enough" began to take root.

Do you remember the poem, "Good Enough" by Edgar A. Guest? I do. I remember in fourth grade being asked to memorize and recite it for a speech:

My son, beware of "good enough,"
It isn't made of sterling stuff;
It's something any man can do,
It marks the many from the few,
It has not merit to the eye,
It's something any man can buy,
Its name is but a sham and bluff,
For it is never "good enough."

At one level, Guest's admonition toward excellence in what we do is a needed admonition against laziness and halfhearted efforts in life. But what can also happen is that a well-intended sentiment becomes an internal narrative that drives our pursuit of who we are.

Nothing less than the best will ever be "good enough" to confirm and maintain my sense of who I am. No amount of "niceness," academic accolades, athletic letters on my jacket, or short-term mission trips will satisfy our deepest need to be saved from ourselves.

The last stanza of Guest's poem closes:

For this is true of men and stuff—
Only the best is "good enough."

What a blessing we have in the gospel that reminds us that we will *never* be good enough, but that through Christ we get something even better than the best—we receive the righteousness of Jesus Christ!

How Can Parents Help?

Speak to the heart

For children who find their identity in their actions and behaviors, getting to the heart behind those actions will be of critical importance for the parent. How might we do this? If your kids are anything like mine, mini-sermonettes about biblical anthropology rarely move the needle in conversations like this. No, I've found many parents have to reclaim and redeem ordinary moments of conversation with their child. Parents can be mindful of some of these factors:

- **Setting:** *Where am I trying to have these conversations?* I find that setting is so important when talking to kids. For instance, one of the settings where I have found a lot of traction for talks like this is in the car on the way to school. For my two older children, I get about ten to fifteen minutes every morning in the car with them (sometimes up to thirty or thirty-five if there's traffic, but that's another story). Fifteen minutes of conversation over five days is seventy-five minutes of conversation. Multiply that over a month, and I've got three hundred minutes (five hours) of conversation! Take five hours of conversation over nine months, and I have roughly forty-five hours of conversation that can be reclaimed. Now, do I take every minute in the car to talk to my kids about their heart and identity? No, of course not! But, those precious minutes in the carpool line can be redeemed for good!
- **Time:** *When am I trying to have these conversations?* When your kid first gets home from school and needs time to recuperate? Is that when you do it? Or first thing in the morning, as they're groggily grabbing the cereal box from the pantry? Proverbs reminds us that there is wisdom in a timely spoken word (Proverbs 15:23). As parents, are we putting our best foot forward by finding a time to speak to our kids that is *best for them* and not

most *convenient for us?* Isn't that a way we can practically love them?

- **Circumstances:** *What is going on in their world right now?* Knowledge of your child's world is critically important here. Are they going through a rough patch at school with academics? Have they experienced hardship in a friendship? Are they disappointed by their performance on the athletic fields? If so, that might inform and shape how you go about your conversations with your kids.
- **Tone:** *How do I speak to them?* Kids are smart. Kids are intuitive. They can smell a fake and condescending conversation a mile away. I know from experience, trust me! There are times when I will use language and tone that my kids roll their eyes at and say, "Dad, stop trying to counsel us like one of your clients." If I come in with a tone that is filled with superiority or condescension, I find I don't get too far. But if my posture is one of openness, curiosity, and kindness, I find that my kids tend to open up. All the time? Of course not; they're kids after all. Again, the Proverbs are helpful here too. Proverbs 16:21 reminds us that "sweetness of speech increases persuasiveness." I want to be as persuasive with my kids as possible, and that starts with my tone!

With those factors in mind then, what are some questions we can ask that push us to the heart of our child? If the heart is the seat of our loves, values, desires, and wants (Proverbs 4:23), then that is what I aim to know.

- Tell me a little bit about why you think you need to do all these activities?
- Who is putting that pressure on you, do you think?
- What kind of internal talk or narrative goes through your mind in relationship to these activities?
- Do you feel like Mom and I expect too much from you? Why or why not?

- What's the worst that could happen if you didn't do all
  _____?
- Do you feel like God wants you to do all these things to please him?
- Have you ever thought about just quitting it all because it's just too much?
- Do you ever get tired or exhausted of doing what you are doing? If so, what do you think that means?

Now, these might seem like "counselor-y" type questions, so of course, feel free to adapt. They're starting points. Remember, in conversation, incentivize vulnerability. When I press my children for answers and engagement with conversation, I try to offer affirmation and praise for their responses. If you immediately jump in with quick fixes, personal anecdotes, or correction, you'll inevitably shut your child down, not open them up. Additionally, don't feel pressure to do all of this in one conversation. One chat might be you listening. Another chat might be you following up on the previous one. A friend of mine is fond of saying, "Don't try and squeeze hundred-dollar conversations into dime-sized moments."

Live out the gospel

Don't tune me out here! I know there are scores of books out there on living the gospel-centered life. But we shouldn't tune that gospel language out because we've heard it so often. As J. C. Ryle cautions us, "Familiarity with sacred things has a dreadful tendency to cause men to despise them."[3] We must never get tired of the gospel. It is good news not just for eternal life, but for everyday life.

Parents, we must live out the good news with our children. As Tim Keller said, "The gospel is this: We are more sinful and flawed in ourselves than we ever dared believe, yet at the very same time we are more loved and accepted in Jesus Christ than we ever dared hope."[4]

How can we live this out with our kids? Consider some of these possibilities:

- When was the last time you held back a consequence for an action and instead showed mercy?
- When was the last time you offered something undeserved and unmerited in a display of grace?
- Do you only affirm and praise good behaviors and actions and punish bad behaviors and actions?

Sally Lloyd-Jones puts it beautifully in her book, *Thoughts to Make Your Heart Sing*:

> What words does God want you to treasure
> in the deepest part of you?
>
> "Be good"? "Do it better"? "Try harder"?
> Are those the words God wrote in the Bible
> for us, to rescue and free us?
>
> No. Those words only show us what we
> can't do.
>
> The words God wants us to remember are
> just three small ones: "I love you!"[5]

BRINGING IT ALL TOGETHER

Of all the different identity struggles children face, this is perhaps the most difficult of them to pin down. I mean, what parent doesn't want a child who obeys, is compliant, respectful, and a rule-follower? Some of you might be nodding your head and saying, "I'll take one of those, please." Yet Scripture reminds us so poignantly,

> "None is righteous, no, not one;
> no one understands;
> no one seeks for God.
> All have turned aside; together they have become worthless;

> no one does good,
> not even one." (Romans 3:10–12)

The inherent lie in all the various identity struggles that we have covered is that *we*, the individual, get the final say on who we are. The lie of autonomy is a dangerous one, and it's also an exhausting one. If we alone must merit and earn our sense of identity, we'll exhaust ourselves trying to do it. Instead of resting in the words and voice of the One who tells us who we are, we'll depend on our morals, our virtues, and our values to earn our spot before the Lord.

The traditional way of forging one's identity depended on hearing, "Well done, good and faithful son/daughter." Our parents' approval was what we yearned for.

But what do you do when your parents are not good? What if they withhold their approval? What if they're impossible to please? For the moralist, this forms an impossible scenario— how much is enough to please their parents and the Lord and when do they know they have done enough?

Such a process of identity formation is fraught with impossibility and exhaustion, which is why the call of a gospel identity is so necessary for the one caught in the trap of their good works. What other message compares to the message Paul shares the following:

> For our sake he made him to be sin who knew no sin, so
> that in him we might become the righteousness of God.
> (2 Corinthians 5:21)

What a relief for our children to know that the perfect obedience of Christ can be theirs through faith and trust in him.

Part 3
I Am What I Feel

Chapter 6
Juan and Gender

Juan is eight years old and headed into the second grade. He loves his family, school, and teachers. Juan's mother is divorced, and his father remarried and lives three hours away. Juan wishes he could see his dad more, but most days he is content to be at home with his mom and two older sisters.

When Juan was around five or six years old, his mother, Rosa noticed that he loved playing dress-up and house with his sisters, Mia and Gina. She didn't think much of it all, but now that he's getting older she has started to be concerned. The other day Mia snapped a photo of Juan in a dress and posted it on her Snapchat. One of Mia's friends commented that he looked so cute and asked Mia if he wanted to be a girl.

Mia replied that she didn't think so, but it did make her curious. The next day, Mia asked Juan if he wanted to be like her and Gina—a girl—to which Juan enthusiastically replied, "Yes!" When Mia relayed this to her mom, her mom told Mia that she needed to cut it out. That night, alone with her thoughts, Rosa wondered if this was the first step toward Juan being confused about his gender. She thought about texting Juan's father, but she knew that wouldn't go anywhere so she went to bed agitated and helpless.

Over the past few years, I have heard more and more stories like Rosa's. Stories of parents who are covering the gamut of topics: peer pressure to identify a certain way, desires to wear opposite gender clothing, or a desire to rename themselves in light of something they read or heard on social media.

There are few topics that elicit more passionate responses, opinions, and bewilderment than gender identity. While space and time do not allow us to delve deeply into this topic, let's talk about some of the basics when it comes to understanding gender, gender identity, and how to help a child live faithfully as God designed and intended them to live.

Understanding the Landscape of Gender Identity

Language and terms in this area of our culture consistently change, thus my encouragement would be to stay as current with language and terminology *as it is helpful for your particular context.* Here are some basic terms that are helpful to be aware of as a parent (you can refer to the glossary on page 105 for additional terms as well):

- *Biological sex*: male or female according to chromosomes (XX—female, XY—male), external/internal physiology (anatomy)
- *Gender*: the psychological, social, and cultural manifestations of maleness and femaleness (masculinity and femininity)
- *Gender identity*: how a person perceives or experiences themselves as male/female[1]

Historically speaking, those three elements (biological sex + gender + gender identity) have aligned for most individuals. In other words, if a person had XY chromosomes and a male anatomy, people saw him as a boy or man, and that is how he saw himself. And if a person had XX chromosomes and a female anatomy, people saw her as a girl or woman, and that is how she saw herself. Currently, the term that is used to describe when those three terms align is *cisgender*.

- *Cisgender*: someone whose gender identity is the same as the sex they were assigned at birth

In the past under a traditional identity framework, people widely assumed that biological sex, gender, and gender identity aligned for everyone. With the advent of expressive individualism (discussed in chapters one and two), one's gender identity does not need to be rooted in one's physical embodied gender but is located in one's own feelings and perceptions of themselves. This change has given rise to more terms that may be unfamiliar but that are helpful to understand.

- *Gender dysphoria*: the experience of incongruence between one's biological sex and gender identity (duration of at least 6 months)[2]
- *Gender confusion, distress, incongruence*: a less-technical term than gender dysphoria that expresses a confusion or sense of distress that a child may have about his/her gender identity
- *Transgender or trans*: broad umbrella term for a person who experiences a different gender identity than their biological sex. Please note that when a person identifies as transgender, it does not necessarily mean that they have changed their style of dress, that they are taking hormones, or that they have had surgery (or plan to have surgery).
- *Gender-fluid*: gender identity best described as a dynamic mix of boy and girl. A person who is gender-fluid may always feel like a mix of the two traditional genders, but may feel more man some days, and more woman other days
- *Gender nonconforming/genderqueer*: A broad term referring to people who do not behave in a way that conforms to the traditional expectations of their gender, or whose gender expression does not fit neatly into a category
- *Gender-affirming care*: A broad term that refers to professional and medical care that affirms and reinforces a child or teen's desired gender identity

A note on ROGD (Rapid Onset Gender Dysphoria)

ROGD is a term that was coined by doctor and researcher, Dr. Lisa Littman. In a peer-reviewed study of parents and children (83 percent female), Dr. Littman noted a cluster of factors beginning to emerge from groups of girls who were coming out as trans:

1. Few of the children showed any signs of gender dysphoria to their parents while growing up.
2. Their new identity seemed to appear out of the blue.
3. Many if not all of their friends at school were trans, and their coming out often followed their friends' coming out as trans.
4. Many of them became more popular after they came out as trans.
5. They engaged in heavy online and social media activity surrounding their coming out.
6. Many of them had other mental health concerns that weren't being dealt with.[3]

Dr. Littman's research and subsequent writing on this topic can be helpful for parents to understand. For some parents, a child's questioning of their gender comes out of left field. The child might come "armed" with an array of data and studies to back up his/her claims. It can feel disorienting for the parent, who, up to that point had no idea their child was struggling.

Contrast ROGD with traditional gender dysphoria in that gender dysphoria is "marked by persistent dysphoria from early childhood," whereas ROGD is "marked by a sudden onset in teens who have never before experienced discomfort with their gender."[4] This is one of the reasons why it is important for parents to be aware of the influences surrounding their child and teen. Considerations around social media, schooling options, and friendships will need to be evaluated.[5]

Abigail Shrier, author of *Irreversible Damage: The Transgender Craze Seducing our Daughters*, echoes and confirms many points of Dr. Littman's research. Shrier notes that historically gender dysphoria only impacted a very small population (roughly .01%) and almost exclusively males. She also notes that prior to 2012 there was little to no scientific literature on girls (ages 11–21) struggling with gender dysphoria at all.[6]

One of the reasons why it's important to know what these terms mean is that more and more people—especially young people—are changing the way they choose to identify. Understanding and acknowledging the landscape is one step toward having engaged and informed conversations with your child. Let's take a look at some statistics.

Statistics

In 2011, the Williams Institute at UCLA surveyed the US population and determined that the adult trans population stood at .3% (roughly 700,000 people). That number doubled in 2016 to .6% (or roughly 1.4 million people).[7] Recently, in 2022 Gallup conducted a national poll that put the adult LGBTQ+ population at 7.1% (double the number when Gallup first measured it in 2012). Trans people account for 10% of the total LGBTQ+ population.[8]

How many children are coming out as transgender? The data on this is notoriously difficult to ascertain. One can imagine that there are times when children might express dislike or discomfort with a particular toy or piece of clothing (if your kids are like mine, this can happen on a daily basis), but that does not mean they are experiencing gender dysphoria. It simply could be that kids are notoriously fickle, and their feelings change. This is where using the official language of gender dysphoria might inadvertently escalate the problems a child is having as opposed to describing what they're feeling as distress, confusion, discomfort, or even incongruence.

Apply that same dynamic to something as important as gender, and you can see why getting consistent statistics on this topic could prove challenging and nearly impossible. In 2016, the *New York Times* writes, "No one knows for sure. Researchers have not figured out how to obtain consistent, reliable answers from teenagers, much less younger children. The best estimates are that the population is small, probably under 1 percent of adolescents."[9] In 2022, the venerable newspaper estimated the population to be roughly at 300,000 children (ages 13–17).[10]

Treatment and Protocols

What happens when children and teenagers come out as transgender? Some of them will seek gender-affirming care. Over the last decade there has been a tremendous spike in children and teens seeking to access such care. Abigail Schrier notes that there has been a 1,000–5,000 percent (yes, that is thousand!) increase in white, teen girls seeking gender-affirming care.[11] In the United Kingdom there has been a 1,460 percent increase for males, and a 5,337 percent increase for females compared to ten years ago.[12]

Statistically speaking, researchers note that most children will ultimately resolve gender confusion and dysphoria on their own. Former Johns Hopkins doctor, Dr. Paul McHugh notes that "70%–80% spontaneously lost those feelings" over time.[13] Former *NY Mag* journalist and podcaster Jesse Singal writes, "At the moment there is strong evidence that even many children with rather severe gender dysphoria will, in the long run, shed it and come to feel comfortable with the bodies they were born with."[14]

As a parent, it is helpful to know what is being recommended to our children who are experiencing gender dysphoria. Dr. Daniel Dionne, a medical doctor and certified biblical counselor, noted a five-fold process that is typically followed when children seek gender-affirming care:

1. Social affirmation
2. Puberty blockers (e.g., Lupron-intermuscular injection)
3. Cross-sex hormones (estrogen/testosterone)
4. Gender-affirming surgery
5. Legal affirmation process (e.g., changing the gender listed on their birth certificate, driver's license, etc.)

Understanding the struggle

Other common questions that come up in my conversation with parents seek to understand what causes or prompts gender confusion and dysphoria amongst children: Why do some children innately seem to accept their biological sex while others express discomfort? Is it genetic? Is it because of the child's family of origin?

Similar to sexual orientation, there is not unanimity on this issue. *Atlantic* journalist Hannah Rosin writes, "For the transgender community, born in the wrong body is the catchphrase that best captures this moment. It implies that the anatomy deceives where the brain tells the truth; that gender destiny is set before a baby takes its first breath. But the empirical evidence does not fit this argument so neatly."[15]

Research scientist Milton Diamond says his study of identical transgender twins shows the same genetic predisposition that has been found for homosexuality: if one twin has switched to the opposite sex, there is a 50-percent chance that the other will as well. But his survey has not yet been published, and no one else has found nearly that degree of correlation.[16] Similarly, Eric Villain, a geneticist at UCLA who specializes in sexual development and sex differences in the brain, says the studies on twins are mixed and that, on the whole, "there is no evidence of a biological influence on transsexualism yet."[17] That is quite different from what one might hear in the mainstream news where one hears that there is scientific and empirical data behind people identifying as the opposite gender.

Midwestern Seminary professor J. Alan Branch concludes, "No one knows what causes gender dysphoria. No one has discovered a transgender gene. No one has discovered a transgender brain. What have been found are some variables that correlate with a higher incidence of transgenderism in certain cases. But no biological or genetic trait has been found that is both necessary and sufficient to cause transgenderism."[18]

At the end of the day, parents must rely on the resources provided through Scripture and the Spirit to thoughtfully ask questions and probe where needed. This could and may often entail seeking the help of a trusted, biblical/Christian counselor whose views on this issue align with yours. Ultimately, causality as it relates to this issue often becomes secondary to caring for the child in front of you.

HOW CAN PARENTS HELP?

As a parent of a child who is struggling with gender confusion, it can seem overwhelming and intimidating to address this issue.[19] What can you do in the face of such a challenge? What can Rosa, Juan's mother, do in the face of such a challenge?

Be mindful of your own emotions and feelings

I find that children are incredibly intuitive as it relates to their parents' emotions. In my work with parents, I find parents gravitate toward one of two extremes in these discussions: underreaction or overreaction. What does an underreaction look like? Well, a child might express ongoing and increasing discomfort and dissonance with their body and gender identity. In response you might say to yourself, "This is just a phase he's going through," or "I think she'll probably just grow out of it." Instead, what could it look like to engage your child's gender distress with compassion and biblical truth?

In my experience, an overreaction is a more common occurrence amongst parents. If a child expresses any gender dissonance, it can be easy to overreact. Many parents want to address these issues immediately and swiftly. A parent's emotional posture during this time can come across and be experienced as fearful, embarrassed, or anxious. Imagine for a moment how your child *might* interpret those emotions. If they feel like you just want to fix them, or if they perceive that they are embarrassing you, would they want to open up, discuss, and connect? Most likely, no. In those moments of difficulty and awkwardness, cry out to the Lord for mercy. It can be easy for parents to forget that they have a Savior and Shepherd who promises to draw near to them in times of trouble and hardship.

Additionally, it's important to be clear about what constitutes gender confusion in the first place. I find many parents find themselves distressed when their son or daughter begins playing with "opposite-gender" toys or chooses to dress in more unisex clothing. Samuel Ferguson notes,

> Parents of young children shouldn't anxiously think that a son or daughter is struggling from gender dysphoria simply because the child doesn't conform to typical gender norms. After all, many modern ideals about masculinity and femininity are more cultural stereotype than biblical truth. Stereotypes can create unnecessary confusion and pressure for children as they grow up. The Bible offers contours for gender expression, especially in relation to sex and marriage but says less than we might think about male and female preferences. Scripture doesn't say men must like sports and hunting or be unemotional.
>
> Nor does the Bible tell us that little girls must wear pink, enjoy dolls, and avoid rough-and-tumble play. If a girl likes karate, excels in math, and prefers short hair, this doesn't mean she's a boy. And if a boy likes dance, excels in art, and grows his hair out, this doesn't mean he's a girl.[20]

Sometimes in our own emotional distress as parents, we might create an environment that pushes a child to think something is wrong with their gender simply because of more culturally informed stereotypes surrounding gender rather than Scripture itself.

Ask questions

So much of our discipleship and leading of our children flourishes as we draw our children out (Proverbs 20:5) and engage their hearts through dialogue and conversation. In our conversations with our children, questions tend to open them up, while answers and problem-fixes tend to shut them down. For example, imagine with me how Rosa might respond in a "problem-fixing" approach:

- Scold Juan for wearing his sister's dress-up clothes.
- Tell him that boys his age are "too old for that kind of thing."
- Make him go play with a boy down the road.
- Punish him if she catches him doing that kind of thing again.

Now contrast that with how Rosa might approach Juan in a question-asking approach:

- "Juan, when your sisters asked you the other day if you wanted to be a girl, what did you say? Tell me a little bit about why you said that?"
- "What do you enjoy in hanging out and playing with your sisters?"
- "Do you think there is something about being a girl that is better than being a boy, like you?"
- "Are there certain feelings or thoughts you are having that you want to talk to me about?"
- "Is there something I can pray for you about?"

Again, questions like this must be contextualized for your own particular situation. As parents, we want to avoid having our child feel that they are going through a police interrogation. Notice that before any *correction* gets offered, *connection* happens first. Connect before you correct. Well-known detransitioner (see definition in the glossary on page 105) Keira Bell notes how misguided she was as a child:

> I was adamant that I needed to transition. It was the kind of brash assertion that's typical of teenagers. What was really going on was that I was a girl insecure in my body who had experienced parental abandonment, felt alienated from my peers, suffered from

anxiety and depression, and struggled with my sexual orientation.

We are told these days that when someone presents with gender dysphoria, this reflects a person's "real" or "true" self, that the desire to change genders is set. But this was not the case for me. As I matured, I recognized that gender dysphoria was a symptom of my overall misery, not its cause.[21]

Implicit in Keira's comment is that the kind and persistent intrusion of parental love through question-asking might have uncovered deeper realities at play in her gender confusion, rather than defaulting to her preferred reality.

Discern what is causing the gender distress, confusion, or incongruence

When speaking and building relationship with your child, seek to understand what might be beneath the gender confusion and discomfort. For instance, Juan might say he wants to be a girl because he wants to be like his sisters. Here the perceived gender confusion might be as simple as his conceptualization that being a girl helps him have a better relationship with his sisters, since he'd be *like* one of his sisters.

In other situations, the discomfort might be a bit deeper. A young girl is uncomfortable with what she perceives are cultural expectations of girls. I had one young woman who was experiencing some gender confusion, and the way she summed it up was, "I don't like the drama, the gossip, the preoccupation with their looks." In this particular case, this young woman ultimately wasn't reacting against *being* an embodied female, but the particular ways that femininity was being expressed at her school. She later commented she felt more comfortable with her guy friends who played sports. The idea that she could play sports *and* be feminine was something that hadn't occurred to her.

What else might be underneath the proverbial iceberg of your child's gender discomfort? Here are some ideas and lines of conversation you could follow up on:

- "Are there certain people that share your gender that you don't like? Are some of these feelings in response to them?"
- "Do you have certain interests, hobbies, or desires that you believe don't belong with your given gender?"
- "Do you feel pressure to look, dress, or style yourself in a particular way?"
- "Are there certain privileges and benefits that you believe someone of the opposite gender enjoys that you wish you had too?"
- "Do you think it would be easier if you were a boy/girl? Why or why not?"
- "Is it possible that something else is causing some of your discomfort and confusion rather than you feeling as if you're in the wrong body?"

It is key to understand at this point that experiencing gender discomfort is not in and of itself sinful. Andrew T. Walker writes, "It is vital to pause here to make very clear a distinction between experiencing an unwanted feeling and acting on a feeling. . . . individuals who experience gender dysphoria are not sinning when such experiences occur. To feel that your body is one sex and your self is a different gender is not sinful. The Bible nowhere categorizes unwanted psychological distress as sinful in itself."[22] Gender dysphoria, distress, or discomfort are all reflective of the broken world we live in. Helping your child understand this can help them open up to you about questions they have or problems they feel with their body.

Talk about gender positively

When we disciple our children in the way of the Lord, we will seek to portray him as Scripture reveals him. In the opening

Scripture, we see that when God creates Adam and Eve—male and female—this is seen as something *very good*. The gendering of our bodies is a good gift from God that displays his plan for human flourishing.

The late professor Howard Hendricks reminds us, "We should not be ashamed to discuss what God was not ashamed to create."[23] Remember, if you're uncomfortable in discussing these things, your kids will pick up on that. They will begin to interpret gender and related confusion/conversation about that as something that causes you discomfort. What if our children heard, saw, and experienced us talking about gender and sexuality as a positive gift from the Lord?

Viewing gender as a gift from the Lord opens up new opportunities for discussion with your child. Rather than their gender being something that is malleable and open to interpretation, a gift is to be received and received with thankfulness and gratitude to the Giver. Marty Machowski, in his helpful children's book *God Made Boys and Girls: Helping Children Understand the Gift of Gender*, writes, "The last thing God made was a boy and a girl to look after the world and take care of it. He made them to be partners in caring for his world and in filling the world with boys and girls just like them!"[24] God's gift of gender was a part of his creative, creation plan to fill the world with his image-bearers. Rather than being something restrictive, gender in God's plan is an invitation to celebrate our God. Listen to David's words in Psalm 139:

> For you formed my inward parts;
>> you knitted me together in my mother's womb.
> I praise you, for I am fearfully and wonderfully made.
> Wonderful are your works;
>> my soul knows it very well.
> My frame was not hidden from you,
> when I was being made in secret,
>> intricately woven in the depths of the earth.
> Your eyes saw my unformed substance;

in your book were written, every one of them,
 the days that were formed for me,
 when as yet there was none of them.
 How precious to me are your thoughts, O God!
 How vast is the sum of them! (Psalm 139:13–17)

Consider the pronoun and name issue

The issue of pronouns and names are some of the most contentious issues in the gender identity conversation. At the end of the day, parents before the Lord must make the wisest decision that they believe is faithful to Scripture. This will require reading and understanding Scripture, walking in the Spirit, praying without ceasing, and seeking the wise counsel of others.

My personal conviction and belief is that for children and teens who remain in the home, it is imperative that parents use the given name of their child and the pronouns that reflect their child's biological sex and embodied gender. We want to parent with God's goals and purposes in mind, even when that might be at odds with what our children say they want.

Pastor Todd Wagner comments, "For starters, if you have kids yourself, be a parent. It's your job to be the adult. Children will be childish, by definition. They think like, well, children (1 Corinthians 13:11). They are not reliably knowledgeable, reasonable, or wise. They lack life experience, a firm grasp of reality, and the ability to make decisions of ultimate importance. In fact, they're not legally allowed to make any major decisions on their own, and any such agreements they try to enter into aren't binding.[25]

Parents' first and primary responsibility is to the Lord, not to the desires of their children. Author Nancy Pearcey writes, ". . . the way to love people is by supporting their *telos*—what is genuinely good for them in light of the way God designed us to function and flourish."[26]

How can parents navigate this potential conversation? One path that can prove helpful is by demonstrating empathy and understanding of your child's situation, while holding to your biblical beliefs. Parents can empathize with the *concerns* and *confusion* of their child, but not share their child's *conclusions* about how to resolve them. At the end of the day, this issue is something parents should seek wisdom and counsel from local church leaders about a contentious, cultural issue.

Entrust to the Lord

Finally, a word to parents who are weary and troubled about their child's gender confusion. These are weighty and hard issues. I have labored and counseled many parents who have felt as if their world was turned upside down when their child opened up to them about their gender confusion. One tendency worried parents have when a child expresses gender confusion and discomfort with their gender identity is to turn the conversation to themselves, away from the child. Their reactions may look like these:

- "How could you do this to me?"
- "I'll never have grandchildren now!"
- "What am I supposed to tell your grandparents?"
- "This is so gross; how could you be thinking like this?"
- "Just so you know, we're not paying for any hormone treatments or surgeries!"

Those are all statements I have heard well-intentioned parents make to their child. And they all make the parent the focus of the conversation, not the struggle of the child. The temptation to do this is understandable, given the magnitude of the issue and the distress the families feel.

But aren't times of distress and trouble some of the sweetest opportunities to draw near to the Lord? The Lord knows, sees, and hears our struggles (even before we speak them!). He is concerned about what we are going through. He calls us to cry out to him in trouble, and he promises to incline his ear to our neediness. There are few things in parenting that push parents to their knees more than struggles like this.

What should parents do then in times like this? It is for us to rightly entrust our child to the Lord. Their gender, their struggle, and their future. Children are a stewarded gift to us; we do not own our kids; they belong to the Lord. Like David in Psalm 131, we acknowledge our fundamental limitation and inability to change hearts and minds and so we rest in the sovereign, loving, tender care of our Lord.

> O Lord, my heart is not lifted up;
>> my eyes are not raised too high;
> I do not occupy myself with things
>> too great and too marvelous for me.
> But I have calmed and quieted my soul,
>> like a weaned child with its mother;
>> like a weaned child is my soul within me.
> O Israel, hope in the Lord
>> from this time forth and forevermore. (Psalm 131)

BRINGING IT ALL TOGETHER

Nowhere does the allure of modern identity's self-declared right to be who you want to be come into view more than in the issue of gender identity. Fifty years ago, a fifteen-year-old child who said, "I'm a boy trapped in a girl's body" would have been met with a few snickers, a couple of laughs, and at a least a concerned look from the parent. Fast-forward to today, where that same fifteen-year-old could repeat, "I'm a boy trapped in a girl's body," and he or she would be taken seriously and with a high level of concern.

Today many in our culture would rush to affirm such a misguided notion. But as parents, we must ask ourselves if encouraging a child's right to identify as whatever gender they choose to be is truly the most loving thing to do. My goal is to teach and talk, train and tutor my child in the ways of the Lord. Using Deuteronomy 6 as my guide, I utilize every means possible— every time and opportunity possible—to help my child become the image-bearer of God he/she is designed to be. This is the task of parental discipleship. This is the task you and I are called to.

Klyne Snodgrass elaborates, "The discussion of Christian identity does not suggest that we engage in some super spiritual task; it urges that we engage in the task of becoming human. Are we not human already? At one level, yes, but being human is both a reality and a process, both a gift of God and a responsibility, a task to be performed with God, for we cannot be fully human apart from relation with God. Identity is a 'God thing' and it must be lived. Identity and identity seeking are about discipleship."[27]

As you and I parent our children through the often difficult waters of gender dysphoria and dissonance, we seek not to squelch their agency and humanity, but rather find the ways in which their biologically sexed, gendered bodies are a gift from the Lord to be used by him as they become fully human.

Chapter 7
Isabella and Sexuality

Isabella walked down the hallway clutching her stack of books. Head down, she headed to her third-period class, World Languages, and accidentally bumped into Jake, one of the offensive lineman for the school football team.

"Watch where you're going, dyke," Jake yelled out.

Rushing into the bathroom, Isabella locked herself in the stall and started to cry. All of this started four weeks ago when Isabella's friends started pressing her to come out. Mallory, one of Isabella's oldest and closest friends had recently come out as gay. Isabella didn't know exactly how to handle it, and as her friends started to ask if she and Mallory were dating, Isabella didn't know how to answer.

Had she and Mallory been friends since they were little? Yes! Did she like Mallory? Yes! Did she want Mallory to be her *girlfriend?* No! Isabella was confused. When Mallory and her friend group started pressing her to say whether she was gay, she just shrugged her shoulders and shook her head in a noncommittal way. Jules, one of their mutual friends, exclaimed, "See, you must be bisexual!" Isabella was confused.

UNDERSTANDING THE LANDSCAPE OF SEXUAL IDENTITY

Understanding the current lay of the land as it relates to sexual identity and orientation requires a book in and of itself. Navigating the current range of identities within the LGBTQ+

community is challenging, in part because they seem to be constantly in flux. It seems as if the list of identities that one could select is as endless as our collective imagination.

In a 2022 Gallup poll of adult Americans, 7.1% identified as LGBTQ+. That number has doubled over a decade since Gallup last took their poll. Of that 7.1%, an astonishing 58.2% of them identify as bisexual. This was by far the leading category followed by gay (20.2%), lesbian (13.4%), transgender (8.8%), or other (1.8%).[1] It's also important to note that LGBTQ+ identification is significantly higher amongst Gen Zers (19.7%) and millennials (11.2%) compared to their older peers in Gen Xers (3.3%) and the baby boomers (2.7%).[2]

One of the letters in the acronym that has seen a meteoric rise are people who identify as bisexual. Debby Herbenick, a professor at Indiana University, observes that as awareness around bisexuality has increased, it has made it easier for people to label themselves as bisexual.[3] Ironically, this trend maps on to the modern identity formation process where the individual *believes* they are choosing their own identity, but in reality the culture is influencing them what their identity is.

In a day and age where labels and self-identification are a rite of child or adolescent passage, some are quick to find a label that in and of itself eschews labels. Joe Carter writes, "The phrase 'bi-curious' has come to be used to refer to such people who are 'interested in having a same gender sexual experience without necessarily labeling their sexual orientation as bisexual.'"[4] Increasingly at the counseling center I lead, we find more and more teen girls who are confused when it comes to their sexual identity.

Girls like Isabella often find that they enjoy and desire connecting with their female friends at a deep and emotional level. Increasingly, both boys and girls can easily confuse affection for their friend as attraction for their friend. When that happens, society and their peers can be quick to slap a label on them. But in fact, many of these young people don't really want their friendships romanticized and sexualized.

UNDERSTANDING THE HISTORY OF SEXUAL IDENTITY

The notion that one's sexual orientation was the most important aspect of one's identity is somewhat of a modern notion. In the first two editions of the DSM (*Diagnostic and Statistical Manual*), homosexuality was listed as a disorder. In 1974, that classification was removed from the manual as well as all subsequent editions. French philosopher and historian Michel Foucault in his influential book, *History of Sexuality [1976]* noted that the men who engaged in same-sex relationships with other men did not typically view those behaviors as different from their pursuit of sexual relationships with women. Sex was seen more as an activity they did, not an identity they took on.

David Greenberg in his work, *The Construction of Homosexuality*, observes that it wasn't until the 1960s and 1970s, beginning in the United States and moving to England and Western Europe, that people identified as homosexual.[5] I'm not saying that people throughout history have not struggled with homosexuality, but rather the idea that one's sexual orientation is the primary marker of identity is a product of the modern identity formation process.

David Halperin concurs in his work, *Before Sexuality: Construction of the Erotic Experience in the Ancient Greek World*, adding that homosexuality as a category for understanding or identifying oneself is less than a century old. He writes, "It [homosexuality] was developed to describe something altogether new in history: a very spirited and energetic social/political movement of identity based on same-sex sexual relations and identity."[6]

UNDERSTANDING THE DEVELOPMENT OF SEXUAL IDENTITY

Mark Yarhouse, a Christian psychologist, has done an enormous amount research on this topic, and he speaks about five stages in the sexual identity formation process. I have found these helpful in understanding people's experience, particularly that of children and teens.[7]

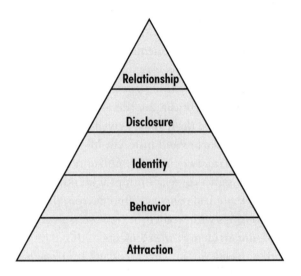

Figure 2. The Development of Sexual Identity

- *Attraction*: At this stage in sexual identity development, the child/teen begins to realize that he/she finds members of the same sex attractive. Arousal and romantic feelings may develop here. This realization in Christian circles is frequently referred to as same-sex attraction (SSA). While attraction and identity are different, our culture promotes that the two are equated and connected.
- *Behavior*: In this stage, the child/teen begins to actively engage in same-sex sexual behavior. One caveat to mention here is that in some cases males will engage in same-sex behavior *without* identifying as gay; while girls might identify as lesbian *before* engaging in same-sex behavior.[8]
- *Identity*: At this point, the child/teen who experiences these attractions (and has potentially engaged in same-sex behavior, see note above) gets to the point of making some sort of "I am _____" statement. It should be noted that not everyone who struggles with same-sex attraction chooses to identity as gay.

- *Disclosure*: In this stage, the child or teen lets other people know about their preferred/chosen identity and experience. This is commonly referred to as "coming out."
- *Relationship*: In this final step, the individual enters into a committed romantic relationship. "A relationship can solidify a person's sense of identity. It can validate so much of what has been in doubt until this point."[9]

UNDERSTANDING THE STRUGGLE

For children and teens who struggle with sexual identity issues, one of the number one questions I receive as a counselor is, "Why does _____ struggle with this? Is it something we have done?" First, that question unintentionally centers the storyline on the parent and not the child. Second, the question, points to an understanding that sexual identity is something that comes about as a result of an action, either by the parent or the child. In my experience counseling teens struggling with their sexual orientation, there is typically not an action that has been done that has been *the* cause for their confusion.

The APA (American Psychological Association) states it like this:

> There is no consensus among scientists about the exact reasons that an individual develops a heterosexual, bisexual, gay or lesbian orientation. Although much research has examined the possible genetic, hormonal, developmental, social and cultural influences on sexual orientation, no findings have emerged that permit scientists to conclude that sexual orientation is determined by any particular factor or factors. Many think that nature and nurture both play complex roles; most people experience little or no sense of choice about their sexual orientation.[10]

So where does that leave parents? Often children and teens might say something like this to their parents, "I was born this way. I can't help how I feel." To which parents often recoil a bit because the idea that "I was born this way" seems so incongruent with their faith. One helpful way to bridge that gap is to ask, "Would it be fair to say that another way to express what you mean here is that *you've always felt this way?*" Many adolescents will assent to this way of putting things. Whether or not there is a biological or genetic factor of being gay, many of them have always felt a same-sex attraction.

To help parents understand this phenomenon, I might ask, "Do you remember a time when you *chose* heterosexuality?" To which many parents smile and shake their heads. You get the picture. Our sexual identity rarely feels like a choice, but more often than not *feels* like an expression of our natural desires. Moreover, as parents we can helpfully remind our children that forming their identity should be based on more than just their sexual attractions. Pastor and author Brad Hambrick notes, "Identity is a choice, one that should be made based on more factors than the persistence of a particular attraction."[11]

We know from the Bible that our desires across the board have been disordered as a result of the fall. Nevertheless, it's important for us to understand what our kids are experiencing.

Here are some things I hear frequently from kids and teens who struggle with their sexual identity:

- "I feel different from everyone else."
- "It's not like I chose this; it's just how I feel."
- "I've never really been good at sports. I've been artistic and musical. That's always been a big difference that I've seen. And I view myself as not as strong as a lot of guys . . . physically. I felt maybe separate from a lot of boys."[12]

Christian counselor Anna Mondal offers a helpful summary, "Scrabbling for causation puts all the emphasis on problem-solving and human reason while de-emphasizing humility and Spirit-dependence."[13] This sentiment is definitely borne out in counseling experience, where parents can spend a lot of time

ransacking the past, thinking through what may or may not
have caused their son or daughter to struggle in this way, and in
doing so, lose valuable opportunities for ministry and discipleship in the present.

Theologian and author Brad Harper, whose son is gay,
addresses the question quite thoughtfully:

> Having talked to dozens of young gay Christian men
> over the years, every one of them has told me, "As soon
> as I realized I had sexual attractions, I realized I was
> attracted to men." Boys do not stand around waiting for
> the school bus one morning and ask themselves, "Okay,
> today I need to decide what I'm going to be—gay or
> straight, gay or straight . . ." Honestly, who would
> choose to be gay, knowing the kind of suffering and
> rejection they would face as a result? I am convinced
> that what a person decides to do with their attractions is
> a choice, but the attractions themselves are not.[14]

In light of this increased awareness and understanding of
the issues surrounding same-sex attraction and sexual identity
confusion, what can parents do for their children and teens?

How Can Parents Help?

Engage with compassion

Let me offer two categories of strugglers here for benefits of
our conversation. One is the category of those who are struggling
with *unwanted* same-sex attraction. These are children and teens
who feel a romantic/sexual attraction to others of the same sex,
but who do not want to have these desires and feelings. Many
of these adolescents are seeking to live in a way that is honoring
to the Lord and adheres to a historic, orthodox understanding
human sexuality.[15] The word that comes to mind in thinking
about these kids is *endurance*. What does faithful endurance look
like in the midst of persistent, unwanted same-sex attraction?

How might I encourage and uplift them in their struggle? How might the words of psalms give voice to their distress and feelings? Consider words like David's in Psalm 57:

> Be merciful to me, O God, be merciful to me,
>   for in you my soul takes refuge;
> in the shadow of your wings I will take refuge,
>   till the storms of destruction pass by.
> I cry out to God Most High,
>   to God who fulfills his purpose for me.
> He will send from heaven and save me;
>   he will put to shame him who tramples on me. Selah
> God will send out his steadfast love and his faithfulness!
> My soul is in the midst of lions;
>   I lie down amid fiery beasts—
> the children of man, whose teeth are spears and arrows,
>   whose tongues are sharp swords.
> Be exalted, O God, above the heavens!
>   Let your glory be over all the earth!
> They set a net for my steps;
>   my soul was bowed down.
> They dug a pit in my way,
>   but they have fallen into it themselves. Selah
> My heart is steadfast, O God,
>   my heart is steadfast!
> I will sing and make melody! (vv. 1–7)

While the context of Psalm 57 is David fleeing from Saul, the point could be made that for many children and teens who struggle with unwanted SSA, their experience can *feel* like an enemy, an unwanted intruder into their life. In the midst of that experience, how can the child and teen cry out to the Lord for mercy and refuge?

A second category of strugglers are those who are experiencing same-sex attraction and believe this is an acceptable life-style for them to build an identity on. In this category, the parent will potentially experience more friction as the difference in approach creates a dissonance in the relationship. The word that comes to mind here builds on our word *endurance* above. That is the word *faithful*. How can parents faithfully point to the truth of God's Word as they engage their child?

Conversations here will be more difficult and contain the potential for the relationship to be broken. Fear of a broken relationship may lead some parents to compromise. But encouraging a child's sinful path is not ultimately loving or compassionate. Parents don't need to choose between loving their children and holding to God's way; it is possible to do both; bearing these principles in mind—beginning with compassion—will give you a start.

Remember that you, parents, play such a key role in these initial discussions. As we've said in earlier chapters, your voice often becomes the dominant voice in your child's internal narrative about who they are. These first conversations surrounding sexual orientation can create a setting that invites more conversation or indicates to your child that no further conversation is desired. Counselor and faculty member, Todd Stryd writes,

> We set the table for the formation of our children's identity by how we talk to them. As parents, we are our child's first window into their self-understanding. Our children take their cues about who they are from the words we use to refer to them and how we talk about them. For good or for ill, how we talk to them becomes the reflexive standard of the way they talk to themselves.[16]

Listen to their perspective

In conversations with my own children, I can be so focused on what I want to say/rebut that I actually miss listening to my children. This danger can appear all too easily in conversations with your child on this topic. Parents come into most conversations deeply convicted and assured of their biblically held values and beliefs (and rightly so!), but in feeling the need to speak all those convictions, we potentially miss out on opportunities for deeper conversation. Let me give you an example:

> Ashtyn: "Can I go over to Morgan's house tonight and spend the night. We have a huge science project we've been working on, and it's due next week."

> Mom: "Ashtyn, we've gone over this a thousand times; you're not going over to her house anymore. I don't know how many times I have to tell you. You're not going to go spend the night at some random girls' house when we know you think you're gay. It's just not going to happen. So, stop asking."

> Ashtyn: "Ugggg, Mom. I can't even. What's wrong with you? I don't even like Morgan. We're just friends, and we need to finish this project up tonight or I'm going to fail the class."

> Mom: "Stop being so dramatic. You know your dad and I don't approve of you being gay. As long as you're in our house you're going to follow and abide by our rules. Period."

> Ashtyn: "This has nothing to do with me being gay. I don't know how many times I have to tell you."

It's a hypothetical conversation, but one I've seen play out in a variety of ways with parents and their children. One of the ironies in sexual identity conversations is that, while we as parents don't want our kids to define their entire identity through the lens of their sexual orientation, we can be guilty of a similar pattern: every conversation with our child gets pushed through the lens of their sexual orientation.

Hear me rightly in this hypothetical case study. I'm not advocating for a lack of discernment or boundaries in allowing or not allowing Ashtyn to spend the night at her friend's house. However, I am advocating for a patient hearing of where Ashtyn is coming from and interacting and engaging those comments/ concerns.

In this moment, it seems that the main concern is that Ashtyn wants to go, work on a project, and spend the evening with her friend Morgan. Engage that question and hear the request. Instead of bringing in the wider conversation regarding Ashtyn's sexual identity, localize the conversation as best as possible. Demonstrate that you are hearing her concern and request.

Know that information rarely changes their position

You'll remember that in chapter 1 we discussed the formation of modern identity. One of the key differences between a modern identity and a gospel-centered identity is that the foundation of a gospel identity is external—what God says about us—whereas the modern identity is founded on subjective truth inside of us. In the modern identity formation process, the main determining factor between right and wrong is not moral, objective truth, but rather how we *feel* in a given situation.

So how did we get here? Psychologist Jonathan Haidt in his book *The Righteous Mind* notes that how we form our ideas about right and wrong, or "moral convictions," has completely changed. Instead of forming our moral convictions on moral absolutes given to us by God, we now make our moral convictions based off a "gut feeling" about what is right and wrong. He calls these gut feelings moral taste buds. In evaluating a given course of action, the modern person asks various questions, three of which are particularly pertinent to the issue of one's sexuality: Does it seem harmful or not harmful? Is it freeing or oppressive? And is it fair or discriminatory? These primary factors, Haidt argues, determine our moral conclusions.[17]

This faulty threefold test explains the disconnect many parents face when speaking to their children about sexual orientation and identity:

- *Test 1*: Is it harmful or not?
  - » "No, being gay, lesbian, or trans doesn't hurt anyone."
- *Test 2*: Is it freeing or oppressive?
  - » "Why would you limit my personal freedom? How or what I identify as is my choice."
- *Test 3*: Is it fair or discriminatory?
  - » "Your ethic does not seem fair. It's repressive and discriminatory."[18]

So, what you can see is that the very way we *do* the conversation surrounding sexual identity rarely makes sense to our children. The argument of the, "Well, the Bible says _____" doesn't move the needle for our children. In our culture, sex is no longer seen as a way to honor God and to create and nurture new human life. Therefore, how one chooses to identify sexually has little to no connection to God, the family, or society. It's ultimately an individual, autonomous choice rooted in their own desires and feelings.

One journalist offers a representative comment on how many people see and view sex, "It's more fun to get [sex] out of the way and see how you connect, and then focus on who they are as a human. 'Are you interesting? Are you fun to be around? Great.' Sex isn't inherently a huge step. At the end of the day, it's a piece of body touching another piece of body—just as existentially meaningless as kissing."[19]

For many children and teens, sex and how you choose to identify is not a big deal. Individuals should be able to identify with whatever sexual orientation they choose and live that truth however they see fit. But do you see the paradox involved here? Identifying as gay or lesbian is a *big deal* (big enough to build an entire identity on), but a *small deal* at the same time (who cares who you love or are romantically attracted to?). What this means for parents is we need to be nimble on our feet in addressing the sexual identity with not only biblical arguments, but also a deep understanding of the cultural waters our kids are swimming in.

One example of those cultural waters is what was discussed in the earlier chapters on identity formation. A key feature of modern identity is that *we are what we feel*. So because I have romantic/sexual feelings for a person of the same gender as my own, I must be gay. One part of parental wisdom will be to hear this line of logic, but ask them to examine that in a deeper way. Is it feasible to define our entire identity on our feelings? Why or why not? Why might this prove to be a shaky and unstable way to figure out who you are?

Engaging your child or teen in dialogue and asking them to play out their conclusions can help them arrive at the right answer rather than you simply offering it to them.

Stay in it for the long haul

In parenting it is said that the days are long, but the years go by fast. I can tell you from current, personal experience that this is true. I often tell parents of children who struggle with SSA or identify as gay or lesbian that they must learn to pray the Lord's Prayer. What do I mean by that? In Matthew 6:10, Jesus encourages the disciples to pray:

"Your kingdom come,
your will be done,
on earth as it is in heaven."

It is easy day in and day out to get discouraged by the perceived lack of progress in these conversations. It is easy to slip into the mentality that our timetable and will is the most important. We grow impatient and frustrated when progress doesn't happen at the speed with which we like. We grow weary and brokenhearted when continued biblical arguments don't make a connection with our children. This is due in large part to our desire for our kingdom agenda to rule the day, rather than submitting our plans to the Lord's.

When it comes to loving and discipling your child or teen, parents must have a long game in perspective. One or two conversations or lectures will not change their chosen path. One mother of an adult son who is gay offers this encouragement and counsel:

> Work hard on your relationship with your child. Be quick to listen and give them the opportunity to talk their thoughts and feelings through with you if they are willing. Be careful not to preach at them; if you've lived your faith before them, they already know what you believe and what God's Word says about sexuality. Remember it's not about you; it's important your child is reassured of your love because they are probably struggling to understand themselves and where they fit in your family and in their world.
>
> It has helped to keep our priorities in order: our job is to love and God's job is to change. My husband and I have made it a priority to keep a strong relationship with our son and his partner so that they know we love them and we hope to influence them toward God by our love for them.[20]

I love how this mother approaches the complexity of the situation. She sacrifices none of her biblical convictions about sexuality and identity, but yet she also does not make this the main point of interaction with her adult son. I've not eavesdropped on a conversation with this mother (I know her personally), but I'm quite confident that there is a range of topics she explores and enjoys speaking with him about: art, culture, movies, music, etc. Her excellent reminder that it is God who changes hearts is one we should not forget.

BRINGING IT ALL TOGETHER

The pressure on the Isabellas of this world to publicly proclaim and be known by their sexual orientation will only increase. This is because our world is obsessed with sex, who you are romantically attracted to, who you are having sex with, and so on. But hidden in that obsession is the pernicious lie that it's better to exchange an identity based on the good words of God—an identity grounded in something truly stable—for an identity that is unstable.

In a traditional identity formation process, sexuality was something rarely discussed, and almost never celebrated. Sexuality was a taboo topic. In a modern identity formation process, our sexuality now becomes the defining feature of our identity. In a gospel identity formation process, the gospel puts both extremes into perspective. Sex is important and plays an important role in God's redemptive story, but it's not worth putting our entire identity in. Here's one way we know Scripture reframes our sexuality in light of his story: Paul in his letter to the Thessalonians offers instruction on how they are to live. He writes,

> Finally, then, brothers, we ask and urge you in the Lord Jesus, that as you received from us how you ought to walk and to please God, just as you are doing, that you do so more and more. For you know what instructions we gave you through the Lord Jesus. For this is the will of God, your sanctification: that you abstain from sexual immorality. (1 Thessalonians 4:1–3)

Do you see what Paul is doing here? He is saying that even how we approach sexuality (either abstaining or engaging in it) is a broader part of our sanctification. Sex is not just something you do or engage in; it is a way that we glorify and honor God.

Additionally, God gets the final word on any sexual expression and activity we engage in because he is the one who created it. When children and teens experience romantic and sexual feelings that are not aligned with God's design, we encourage them to align their actions and behaviors with God's will through obedient living. Our feelings and desires are often persistent in this area, which is why faithful and steady encouragement of parents and godly influences in the child and teenager's life is crucial.

This is not the same as engaging in conversion therapy, which sees homosexuality as a mental disorder. It means living as God designed us, bringing all of our desires to the Lord, and asking for help to walk in a manner worthy of our calling. Stryd writes, "Character formation requires parental decision-making. One of your parental responsibilities is to direct your child toward what is best for them, regardless of whether he or she has a different opinion on the matter."[21]

This is not unkind or unloving to say or hold to. Quite the opposite in fact. How would it be loving or kind to allow an individual to use something that was absolutely contrary to its original design and intention? Theologian and author Kelly Kapic writes, "Because our identity is found in Christ, the problem with our sin is less that we have broken a rule and more that we are not acting according to who we are."[22]

The good news we want to communicate to our children is that they are created by God and that creation extends to their sexual orientation. His voice is the only one that matters in the end. And while the allure of the world and the appeal of the past might be powerful and attractive forces in shaping who we are, who better than the Lord himself to shape and form our child's most fundamental reality of who they are?

Conclusion

Everyone lives and operates out of some narrative identity, whether it is thought out and reflected upon or not.
—Timothy Keller[1]

Recently I got called on for jury duty. Let me tell you, it was quite the education into our judicial and legal system. I think I got a semester's worth of learning in one brief week. As the potential jurors were all filing into the courtroom for *voir dire* (that's the French term for the jury selection process I learned), I had high hopes that I would not be selected. In addition to some pretty good excuses I had lined up to offer the judge, I was one of fifty potential jurors for a jury of twelve. I thought I had this in the bag.

As the lawyers spent time questioning each of us, I raised my hand to let them know I needed to be home for some family coming in from out of town. The lawyers asked a few clarifying questions, but in the end my excuses held no sway. I was still in it. As the lawyers moved down the row, a gentleman in the back raised his hand to offer a reason why he didn't think he could serve on jury duty that week.

When the judge asked him if he could serve, he simply replied, "No."

The judge asked again, "Do you mind if I ask why you can't serve, sir?"

To which the potential juror said, "I just don't want to."

After the judge, somewhat exasperated, looked to counsel and the prosecuting attorney for help, she said, "You're dismissed." Everyone gasped a bit in the courtroom. Really? That easy? All he had to do was say, "I don't want to be here, and he got off?" Let me tell you, people were not happy.

I ended up being selected for jury duty. The gentleman who had been excused from jury duty became infamous in our conversations as "yellow-shirt guy." Comments abounded, "Must be nice to be 'yellow-shirt guy'" or "Guess if you don't want to do something, you just act like 'yellow-shirt guy.'"

That poor fella, who was nameless for obvious reasons, will never know that the only way he was referred to throughout the week was for his eponymous yellow shirt. I seriously doubt that he would have wanted to be known in that banal sort of way. I'm confident there were probably at least a hundred other things that he could be known for—identified by even—and yet "yellow-shirt" was what was chosen for him. His identity, complex as it was, was simplified to something as silly as a shirt.

In a similar way, we've discussed the many and varied ways that our children and teens can find their identity in something other than who God says we are:

- Academic acumen
- Athletic performance
- Moralism and good works
- Gender identity
- Sexual orientation

In each of these categories, a child can wrongly root and base their sense of who they are in an activity (academics, athletics, moralism) or their own feelings and perceptions (gender identity and sexual orientation). What I hope you've seen is that none of these is unimportant in the development of who we are, but none of these should be the primary narratives in building who we are. As Dietrich Bonhoeffer writes, "More important matters are at stake than self-knowledge."[2] What matters is what God thinks of you.

The Heidelberg Catechism, centuries old, holds important clues and truths about this:[3]

Q. What is your only comfort in life and in death?

A. That I am not my own,
but belong—
body and soul,
in life and in death—
to my faithful Savior, Jesus Christ.
He has fully paid for all my sins with his precious blood,
and has set me free from the tyranny of the devil.
He also watches over me in such a way
that not a hair can fall from my head
without the will of my Father in heaven;
in fact, all things must work together for my salvation.
Because I belong to him,
Christ, by his Holy Spirit,
assures me of eternal life
and makes me wholeheartedly willing and ready
from now on to live for him.

In the opening to his book *Who God Says You Are*, Klyne Snodgrass writes, "There is only one question: Who are you? Everything else in life flows from that one question. . . . If your life has any meaning, it will be because you project—and have projected—a meaningful identity."[4] If I can venture one small addition to Snodgrass's question, it is this: not only *who are you*, but *whose are you*. Who do you belong to? You belong body and soul, in life and death, to our Savior Jesus Christ.

Dr. Judy Cha puts it simply, "Our primary identity is as people distinctly made in God's image, to be his treasured possession, his children to reflect and represent who he is. This truth about us should be the groundwork in which all aspects of our identity are rooted and lived out. Who God says we are gives us unchanging value and worth."⁵

As parents, you will have significant sway in shaping how your child thinks about their identity. In fact, your voice is often one of the most formative voices in their life as they go through childhood, adolescence, and adulthood. With so much influence to steward, how can we as parents rightly serve as the Lord's ambassadors to our children? Speaking the words of the Lord, may we seek to share the good news of our identity that is not based on our performance or abilities or feelings, but solely based on the person and work of Jesus Christ, our Savior and Redeemer!

Glossary

Biological sex: male or female according to chromosomes (XX-female, XY- male), external/internal physiology (anatomy)

Bisexual or bi: someone who can be attracted to more than one gender

Cisgender: someone whose gender identity is the same as the sex they were assigned at birth

Detransitioner/desisting: someone who previously identified as transgender and received medical and/or surgical interventions as a result, but stopped taking these interventions and no longer identifies as transgender in the same way

DSM: *DSM* stands for the *Diagnostic and Statistic Manual*. It is currently in its fifth edition. This manual forms the basis for professional counselors to assess and diagnose individuals.

Gender: the psychological, social, and cultural manifestations of maleness and femaleness (masculinity and femininity)

Gender distress, confusion, incongruence: a less-technical term than gender dysphoria, expressing a confusion or sense of distress that a child may have about his/her gender identity

Gender dysphoria: the experience of incongruence between one's biological sex and gender identity (duration of at least six months)

Gender-fluid: gender identity best described as a dynamic mix of boy and girl (A person who is gender-fluid may always feel like a mix of the two traditional genders, but may feel more man some days, and more woman other days.)

Gender identity: how a person perceives or experiences themselves as male/female (how they understand themselves)

Gender nonconforming/genderqueer: A broad term referring to people who do not behave in a way that conforms to the traditional expectations of their gender, or whose gender expression does not fit neatly into a category

Genderqueer: someone whose gender identity and/or expression falls between or outside of male and female

Gospel identity: an identity that is rooted in the good news of Scripture, an identity that is received, not achieved by our performance or validated by our feelings

Identity formation: a process by which an individual comes to an understanding of who they are

Intersex: those whose sex at birth is somewhat ambiguous; 1 in every 5,000 births (0.02%); people whose chromosomes, genitals, or gonads do not allow them to be distinctively identified as male or female at birth

LGBTQ+: a common acronym used to abbreviate lesbian, gay, bisexual, transgender, queer, and others

Modern identity: an identity that is founded and based primarily around the individual's feelings and self-expression

ROGD (Rapid Onset Gender Dysphoria): refers to a trans identification that first occurs after puberty in an adolescent or young
adult without a childhood experience of gender dysphoria[1]

Sexual identity: Refers to how an individual defines their emotional, physical, and/or romantic attractions. Categories of
sexual orientation include, but are not limited to, gay and lesbian (attracted to some members of the same gender), bisexual
(attracted to some members of more than one gender), and het-
erosexual (attracted to some members of another gender)

Sports performance anxiety: anxiety related to an athlete's performance in a sport; signs of performance anxiety include feelings of weakness, "butterflies" in the stomach, elevated heart
rate, fast breathing, muscle tension, frustration, paralyzing
terror, cold sweat, clammy hands, and negative self-talk

Traditional identity: an identity that is founded and based primarily around one's family of origin and familial expectations

Transgender or trans: broad umbrella term for a person who
experiences a different gender identity than their biological sex
(Please note that when a person identifies as transgender, it does
not necessarily mean that they have changed their style of dress,
that they are taking hormones, or that they have had surgery [or
plan to have surgery].)

W-A-S cycle: worry-anxiety-stress cycle; worried thoughts produce anxious feelings, which result in stressed bodies

Resources for Further Reading

GENERAL IDENTITY

- Timothy Keller, *Making Sense of God: Finding God in the Modern World* (New York City, NY: Viking, 2016).
- Chris Morphew, *Who Am I and Why Do I Matter?* (Good Book Company, 2022).
- Alan Noble, *You Are Not Your Own: Belonging to God in an Inhuman World* (Grand Rapids, MI: Brazos, 2022).
- Brian Rosner, *How to Find Yourself: Why Looking Inward Is Not the Answer* (Wheaton, IL: Crossway, 2022).
- Klyne Snodgrass, *Who God Says You Are: A Christian Understanding of Identity* (Grand Rapids, MI: Eerdmans, 2018).
- Paul Tautges, *Remade: Embracing Your Complete Identity in Christ* (Phillipsburg, NJ: P&R Publishing, 2023).
- Carl R. Trueman, *The Rise and Triumph of the Modern Self: Cultural Amnesia, Expressive Individualism, and the Road to Sexual Revolution* (Wheaton, IL: Crossway, 2020).
- Stephen Viars, *Do You Believe What God Says about You? How a Right View of Your Identity in Christ Changes Everything* (Eugene, OR: Harvest House, 2022).

GENDER IDENTITY

- Samuel D. Ferguson, *Does God Care about Gender Identity? Answer* (Wheaton, IL: Crossway, 2023).
- Marty Machowski, *God Made Boys and Girls: Helping Children Understand the Gift of Gender* (Greensboro, NC: New Growth Press, 2019).
- Brian Seagraves and Hunter Leavine, *Gender: A Conversation Guide for Parents and Pastors* (Good Book Company, 2018).
- Robert S. Smith, *How Should We Think about Gender and Identity?* (Bellingham, WA: Lexham Press, 2022).
- Preston Sprinkle, *Embodied: Transgender Identities, the Church, and What the Bible Has to Say* (Colorado Springs, CO: David C. Cook, 2021).

SEXUAL IDENTITY

- Jennifer Kvamme, *More to the Story: Deep Answers to Real Questions on Attraction, Identity, and Relationships* (Good Book Company, 2024).
- Jenell Williams Paris, *The End of Sexual Identity: Why Sex Is Too Important to Define Who We Are* (Downers Grove, IL: IVP Books, 2011).
- Mark A. Yarhouse, *Understanding Sexual Identity: A Resource for Youth Ministry* (Grand Rapids, MI: Zondervan, 2013).

Acknowledgments

I t takes a village to write a book, of that I am convinced. This book would not exist without the teaching and writing of one individual in particular, and that is Tim Keller. I only met Tim one time in person, but I have spent countless hours with him through his writing, sermons, and teaching. When I first heard Tim teach on identity in 2017, I was blown away. I had never heard such a compelling presentation and a more salient synthesis of the way people come into a sense of who they are. To say I was captivated is an understatement. His fingerprints are all over this book. Anything that is helpful, informative, and enlightening, I credit him; any confusion produced, I happily own.

Additionally, I want to thank my wife, Jennifer, who is always a faithful cheerleader and encourager. Writing a book is a significant investment of time, and I'm grateful for her partnership in this endeavor. To my four girls, for whom I ultimately write this, you have taught me much about being a father. I have learned things from you that have deeply impacted me. Thank you for being patient, good listeners, and allowing me to put on my "counselor hat" with you. I love you all dearly.

To my colleagues at Fieldstone Counseling, thank you for your ongoing encouragement and sharpening. A special thank you to Clair Northcutt who graciously read through the yet-to-be completed manuscript in its early stages. To the family at

New Growth Press, thank you for believing in this project. Rush Witt, Ruth Castle, Barb Juliani, and the entire editing team— thank you for your patient support through this process.

Finally, a special thank you to the scores of parents, counselees, and church workers who provided input through surveys and conversations. I pray I have faithfully reflected your words and spirit in each chapter. For those I have had the privilege of counseling and caring for, please know that you have taught and helped me in ways you will never know. Blessings to you all.

Notes

Chapter 1

1. Brian Rosner, *How to Find Yourself: Why Looking Inward Is Not the Answer* (Wheaton, IL: Crossway, 2022), 11.

2. Todd Stryd, "Forming Christian Identity in Our Children," *Journal of Biblical Counseling* 37, no. 1 (2023): 24.

3. Stryd, "Forming Christian Identity in Our Children," 24.

4. I also readily admit and grieve the reality that this is not always the case for a variety of reasons, e.g., adoption, death of a parent(s), parents who are not able to parent due to mental health issues, substance abuse, etc.

5. Rosner, *How to Find Yourself*, 98.

6. Timothy Keller, Gospel Identity Conference, Redeemer Presbyterian Church, New York, New York, November 17–18, 2017, https://gospelinlife.com/downloads/gospel-identity-conference; Timothy Keller, *Making Sense of God: An Invitation to the Skeptical* (New York: Viking, 2016). I am indebted to the late Timothy Keller for his lucid synthesis of these concepts. Much of what is related here is drawn from these sources.

7. John Stuart Mill, *On Liberty* (London: John Parker and Sons, 1859), 22, https://www.norton.com/college/history/ralph/workbook/ralprs28b.htm.

8. Carl R. Trueman, *The Rise and Triumph of the Modern Self: Cultural Amnesia, Expressive Individualism, and the Road to Sexual Revolution* (Wheaton, IL: Crossway, 2020), 123.

9. Sam Allberry, "Why Nancy Pearcey Wants You to Love Your Body," The Gospel Coalition, March 7, 2018, https://www.the gospelcoalition.org/article/nancy-pearcey-wants-love-body/.

10. Keller, *Making Sense of God*, 134.

11. C. S. Lewis, *Mere Christianity* (1952; repr., Grand Rapids: Zondervan, 2001), 226–27.

12. John Stott, *Basic Christianity* (Grand Rapids: William B. Eerdmans, 2008), 122.

13. Christopher Watkins, *Biblical Critical Theory: How the Bible's Unfolding Story Makes Sense of Modern Life and Culture* (Grand Rapids: Zondervan Academic, 2022), 93.

Chapter 2

1. Timothy Keller, *Making Sense of God: Finding God in the Modern World* (New York: Viking Press, 2016), 139.

2. Keller, *Making Sense of God*, 121.

3. Timothy Keller, Gospel Identity Conference, Redeemer Presbyterian Church, New York, New York, November 17–18, 2017, https://gospelinlife.com/downloads/gospel-identity-conference; Timothy Keller, *Making Sense of God: An Invitation to the Skeptical* (New York: Viking, 2016), 118–32. I am indebted to the late Timothy Keller for his lucid synthesis of these concepts. Much of what is related here is drawn from these sources.

4. Nancy Pearcey, *Love Thy Body: Answering the Hard Questions about Life and Sexuality* (Grand Rapids: Baker Books, 2018), 156.

5. Eliana Dockterman, "Kid of the Year Finalist Cash Daniels, 13, Cleans Up Literal Tons of Trash," *TIME*, February 7, 2022, https://time.com/6128595/kid-of-the-year-finalist-cash-daniels/.

6. Dockterman, "Kid of the Year."

7. Keller, *Making Sense of God*, 101.

8. Wendy Finerman, producer, *The Devil Wears Prada*, directed by David Frankel (20th Century Studios, 2006).

9. @JeremyTreat5, Twitter, September 26, 2019, https://x.com/JeremyTreat5/status/1173624816382795777.

10 Michael Horton, *The Gospel-Driven Life: Being Good News People in a Bad News World* (Grand Rapids: Baker, 2009), 12.

11. Todd Stryd, "Forming Christian Identity in Our Children," *Journal of Biblical Counseling* 37. no. 1 (2023): 27.

12. Judy Cha, *Who You Are: Internalizing the Gospel to Find Your True Identity* (Grand Rapids: Zondervan Reflective, 2023), 71.

Chapter 3

1. Tom Kane and Sean Reardon, "Parents Don't Understand How Far Behind Their Kids Are in School," *New York Times*, May 11, 2023, https://www.nytimes.com/interactive/2023/05/11/opinion/pandemic-learning-losses-steep-but-not-permanent.html.

2. David Murray, *Why Is My Teenager Feeling Like This? A Guide for Helping Teens through Anxiety and Depression* (Wheaton, IL: Crossway, 2020), 121.

3. Tonya Harris, Council of the Great City Schools (Washington, D.C., October 24, 2015), https://www.cgcs.org/cms/lib/dc00001581/centricity/domain/4/testing%20report.pdf.

4. Jessica Thompson, *How to Help Your Anxious Teen: Discovering the Surprising Sources of Their Worries and Fears* (Eugene, OR: Harvest House Publishers, 2019), 32.

5. Raychelle Lohmann, "How Much Homework Is Too Much for Our Teens?," *US News & World Report*, March 20, 2018, https://health.usnews.com/wellness/for-parents/articles/2018-03-20/how-much-homework-is-too-much-for-our-teens. On average per the National PTA and NEA, students should be doing roughly ten minutes of homework per night per grade level.

6. Carinne Downs, interview by the author, August 18, 2023.

7. Carinne Downs, interview by the author, August 18, 2023.

8. David Tripp, *New Morning Mercies: A Daily Gospel Devotional* (Wheaton: Crossway, 2014), 5.

9. Carinne Downs, interview by the author, August 18, 2023.

10. Murray, *Why Is My Teenager Feeling like This*, 121.

11. Chris Morphew, *Who Am I and Why Do I Matter?* (United Kingdom: The Good Book Company, 2022), 34–35.

Chapter 4

1. Chris Doob, "Opinion: The impact of sports on American children's mental health," *CT Post*, November 21, 2022, https://www.ctpost.com/opinion/article/Opinion-The-impact-of-sports-on-American-17595617.php.

2. Sarah Eekhoff Zylstra and Ross Douma, "Why we pulled our kids from club sports," The Gospel Coalition, January 4, 2024, https://www.thegospelcoalition.org/article/pulled-kids-club-sports/.

3. Sara Breidigan, "Sports Performance Anxiety: Preparing Your Child for Optimal Play," Nationwide Children's, September 12, 2019, https://www.nationwidechildrens.org/family-resources-education/700childrens/2019/09/sports-performance-anxiety.

4. Julie Lowe, "When a child says 'I don't know,'" CCEF, April 4, 2016, https://www.ccef.org/when-child-says-i-dont-know.

5. Jessica Thompson, *How to Help Your Anxious Teen: Discovering the Surprising Sources of Their Worries and Fears* (Eugene, OR: Harvest House Publishers, 2019), 8.

6. "How Anxiety Can Affect Sports Performance and How to Combat It," UMPC, May 18, 2022, https://share.upmc.com/2022/05/how-anxiety-affects-sports-performance/.

7. "Children and Teens: Anxiety and Depression," ADAA, 2015 Child Mind Institute Children's Mental Health Report, https://adaa.org/living-with-anxiety/children.

8. "Children and Teens: Anxiety and Depression."

9. "Scholarships," NCAA, https://www.ncaa.org/sports/2014/10/6/scholarships.aspx. Accessed March 4, 2024.

10. Melanie Hanson, "Scholarship Statistics," Education Data Initiative, January 14, 2024, https://educationdata.org/scholarship-statistics.

11. "Probability of Competing Beyond High School," NCAA, https://www.ncaa.org/sports/2013/12/17/probability-of-competing-beyond-high-school.aspx. Accessed 4 March 2024.

12. Corbett Smith, "Time and Money," *Dallas Morning News*, http://res.dallasnews.com/interactives/club-sports/part1/. Accessed January 22, 2024.

13. For example, you can purchase encouraging note cards at https://www.amazon.com/Scripture-Lunch-Notes-cards-Noteworthy/dp/1441335463.

14. Recommendations related to this topic: Collin Hansen, ed., *The New City Catechism Devotional* (Wheaton, IL: Crossway, 2017); David Murray, *Exploring the Bible Together: A 52-Week Family Worship Plan* (Wheaton, IL: Crossway, 2020); Chris Morphew, *Who Am I and Why Do I Matter?* (Epsom, Surrey, UK: The Good Book Company, 2022);

Kristen Hatton, *Face Time: Your Identity in a Selfie World* (Greensboro, NC: New Growth Press, 2017); Marty Machowski, *The Ology: Ancient Truths Ever New* (Greensboro, NC: New Growth Press, 2015).

15. Henri Nouwen, *Who Are We?: Henri Nouwen on Our Christian Identity* (Silver Spring, MD: Learn 25, 2017), Audiobook.

Chapter 5

1. Klyne R. Snodgrass, *Who God Says You Are: A Christian Understanding of Identity* (Grand Rapids: William B. Eerdmans Publishing, 2018), 2.

2. David Strain, "How Union with Christ Shapes Our Identity," *Table Talk Magazine*, July 15, 2022, https://tabletalkmagazine.com/posts/how-union-with-christ-shapes-our-identity/.

3. J. C. Ryle, *Matthew: Expository Thoughts on the Gospels* (Carlisle, PA: Banner of Truth Trust, 2012), 9.

4. Timothy J. Keller with Kathy Keller, *The Meaning of Marriage: Facing the Complexities of Commitment with the Wisdom of God* (New York: Viking, 2011), 48.

5. Sally Lloyd-Jones, *Thoughts to Make Your Heart Sing* (Grand Rapids: ZonderKidz, 2012), 24.

Chapter 6

1. The Human Rights Campaign elaborates on their definition of gender identity, "One's innermost concept of self as male, female, a blend of both or neither—how individuals perceive themselves and what they call themselves. One's gender identity can be the same or different from their sex assigned at birth." From the reading in chapter 1, you can see how gender identity is something that is self-confirmed and identified—a hallmark of modern identity. (https://www.hrc.org/resources/glossary-of-terms)

2. The DSM-V provides a fuller explanation of this diagnosis.

3. Preston Sprinkle, *Embodied: Transgender Identities, the Church, and What the Bible Has to Say* (Colorado Springs: David C. Cook, 2021), 163.

4. Jen Oshman, *Cultural Counterfeits: Confronting 5 Empty Promises of Our Age and How We Were Made for So Much More* (Wheaton, IL: Crossway, 2022), 134.

5. Read here for a fascinating story of one family's journey through gender identity: https://www.thegospelcoalition.org/article/transformation-transgender-teen/.

6. Abigail Shrier, *Irreversible Damage: The Transgender Craze Seducing Our Daughters* (Washington, D.C.: Regnery Publishing, 2020), xxi.

7. Jody L. Herman, Andrew R. Flores, Kathryn K. O'Neill, "How Many Adults Identify as Transgender in the United States?," June 2022, http://williamsinstitute.law.ucla.edu/wp-content/uploads/How-Many-Adults-Identify-as-Transgender-in-the-United-States.pdf.

8. Jeffrey Jones, "LGBT Identification in U.S. Ticks Up to 7.1%," *Gallup News*, February 17, 2022, https://news.gallup.com/poll/389792/lgbt-identification-ticks-up.aspx.

9. Jan Hoffman, "As Attention Grows, Children's Transgender Numbers Are Elusive," *New York Times*, May 17, 2016, https://www.nytimes.com/2016/05/18/science/transgender-children.html.

10. Megan Twohey and Christina Jewett, "They Paused Puberty, but Is There a Cost?" *New York Times*, November 14, 2022, https://www.nytimes.com/2022/11/14/health/puberty-blockers-transgender.html.

11. Joseph Backholm, "Is America really getting gayer?" *World News Mag*, March 16, 2022, https://wng.org/opinions/is-america-really-getting-gayer-1647431229.

12. Sprinkle, *Embodied*, 166.

13. Paul McHugh, "Transgender Surgery Isn't the Solution," *Wall Street Journal*, May 13, 2016, https://www.wsj.com/articles/paul-mchugh-transgender-surgery-isnt-the-solution-1402615120.

14. Jesse Singal, "What's Missing from the Conversation about Transgender Kids," *The Cut*, July 25, 2016, https://www.thecut.com/2016/07/whats-missing-from-the-conversation-about-transgender-kids.html.

15. Hannah Rosin, "A Boy's Life," *The Atlantic*, November 2008, https://www.theatlantic.com/magazine/archive/2008/11/a-boys-life/307059/.

16. Rosin, "A Boy's Life."

17. Rosin, "A Boy's Life."

18. J. Alan Branch, *Affirming God's Image: Addressing the Trans-gender Question with Science and Scripture* (Bellingham, WA: Lexham Press, 2019), 129.

19. Conversely, I know there are also a group of parents who might be reading this who don't find these conversations overwhelming and intimidating but might find themselves desiring to affirm and promote gender-affirming care. My hope and prayer is that some of what might be shared and covered in this chapter will help offer a biblical alternative.

20. Samuel D. Ferguson, *Does God Care about Gender Identity?* (Wheaton, IL: Crossway, 2023), 29–30.

21. Keira Bell, "My Story," *Persuasion*, April 7, 2021, https://www.persuasion.community/p/keira-bell-my-story.

22. Andrew T. Walker, *God and the Transgender Debate: What Does the Bible Actually Say about Gender Identity* (Charlotte, NC: The Good Book Company, 2017), 68.

23. Juli Slattery, *Rethinking Sexuality: God's Design and Why It Matters* (Colorado Springs: Multnomah, 2018), 32.

24. Marty Machowski, *God Made Boys and Girls: Helping Children Understand the Gift of Gender* (Greensboro, NC: New Growth Press, 2019), 15.

25. Todd Wagner, "Talking to Kids about Gender in a Gender-Confused World," The Gospel Coalition, November 15, 2019, https://www.thegospelcoalition.org/article/talking-kids-gender-confused-age/.

26. Nancy Pearcey, *Love Thy Body: Answering the Hard Questions about Life and Sexuality* (Grand Rapids: Baker Books, 2018), 171.

27. Klyne R. Snodgrass, *Who God Says You Are: A Christian Understanding of Identity* (Grand Rapids: William B. Eerdmans Publishing, 2018), 33.

Chapter 7

1. Jeffrey Jones, "LGBT Identification in U.S. Ticks Up to 7.1%," *Gallup News*, February 17, 2022, https://news.gallup.com/poll/389792/lgbt-identification-ticks-up.aspx.

2. Jeffrey Jones, "LGBT Identification in U.S. Ticks Up to 7.1%," *Gallup News*, February 17, 2022, https://news.gallup.com/poll/389792/lgbt-identification-ticks-up.aspx.

3. Carina Storrs, "Bisexuality on the rise, says new U.S. survey," *CNN*, January 7, 2016, https://www.cnn.com/2016/01/07/health/bi sexuality-on-the-rise/index.html.

4. Joe Carter, "Why Teenagers Are Becoming Trans-Curious," The Gospel Coalition, March 5, 2018, https://www.thegospelcoalition .org/article/why-teenagers-are-becoming-trans-curious/.

5. Glenn T. Stanton, *Loving My (LGBT) Neighbor: Being Friends in Grace and Truth* (Chicago: Moody Publishers, 2014), 28.

6. Stanton, *Loving My (LGBT) Neighbor*, 43.

7. Mark A. Yarhouse, *Understanding Sexual Identity: A Resource for Youth Ministry* (Grand Rapids: Zondervan, 2013), 62.

8. Yarhouse, *Understanding Sexual Identity*, 53.

9. Yarhouse, 63.

10. "Answers to Your Questions for a Better Understanding of Sexual Orientation and Homosexuality," American Psychological Association, 2008, http://www.apa.org/topics/lgbt/orientation.pdf

11. Brad Hambrick, *Do Ask, Do Tell, Let's Talk: Why and How Christians Should Have Gay Friends* (Minneapolis, MN: Cruciform Press, 2016), 20.

12. Yarhouse, *Understanding Sexual Identity*, 55.

13. Anna Mondal, "Counseling Gender-Questioning Teens," Biblical Counseling Coalition, January 10, 2020, https://www.biblicalcounseling coalition.org/2020/01/10/counseling-gender-questioning-teens-part-2/.

14. Brad and Drew Harper, *Space at the Table: Conversations Between an Evangelical Theologian and His Gay Son* (Vancouver, WA: Self-Published, 2016), 15.

15. I realize there is a diversity of belief even within the evangelical Christian community on same-sex relationships. For an extended treatment on this topic, these resources are recommended: Kevin DeYoung, *What Does the Bible Really Teach about Homosexuality?* (Wheaton, IL: Crossway, 2015); Sam Allberry, *Is God Anti-Gay? And Other Questions about Homosexuality, the Bible, and Same-Sex Attraction* (Epsom, Surrey, UK: The Good Book Company, 2023); Christopher Yuan, *Holy Sexuality and the Gospel: Sex, Desire, and Relationships Shaped by God's Grand Story* (Colorado Springs, CO: Multnomah, 2018).

16. Todd Stryd, "Forming Christian Identity in Our Children," *Journal of Biblical Counseling* 37, no. 1 (2023): 28.

17. Sam Allberry, "Where to Find Hope and Help amid the Sexual Revolution," The Gospel Coalition, November 5, 2018, https://www.thegospelcoalition.org/article/hope-help-sexual-revolution/.

18. The other three are loyalty/betrayal, authority/subversion, sanctity/degradation.

19. Alex Morris, "Tales from the Millennials' Sexual Revolution," *Rolling Stone*, March 31, 2014. https://www.rollingstone.com/interactive/feature-millennial-sexual-revolution-relationships-marriage/.

20. Marilyn Vaughan, interview by the author, 2023.

21. Stryd, "Forming Christian Identity in Our Children," 34.

22. Kelly M. Kapic, *You're Only Human: How Your Limits Reflect God's Design and Why That's Good News* (Grand Rapids: Brazos Press, 2022), 92.

Conclusion

1. Timothy Keller, *The Reason for God: Belief in an Age of Skepticism* (London: Penguin, 2009), 15.

2. Kelly M. Kapic, *You're Only Human: How Your Limits Reflect God's Design and Why That's Good News* (Grand Rapids: Brazos Press, 2022), 89.

3. "Heidelberg Catechism," Westminster Theological Seminary, https://students.wts.edu/resources/creeds/heidelberg.html.

4. Klyne R. Snodgrass, *Who God Says You Are: A Christian Understanding of Identity* (Grand Rapids: William B. Eerdmans Publishing, 2018), 1.

5. Judy Cha, *Who You Are: Internalizing the Gospel to Find Your True Identity* (Grand Rapids: Zondervan Reflective, 2023), 36.

Glossary

1. Sasha Ayad, Lisa Marchiano, and Stella O'Malley, *When Kids Say They're Trans: A Guide For Parents* (Durham, NC: Pitchstone Publishing, 2023), 22.